Wild Galloway

Wild Galloway

From the hilltops to the Solway,
a portrait of a glen

Ian Carter

Whittles Publishing

Published by
Whittles Publishing,
Dunbeath,
Caithness KW6 6EG,
Scotland, UK

www.whittlespublishing.com

© 2025 Ian Carter
ISBN 978-184995-587-4

All rights reserved.
No part of this publication may be reproduced,
stored in a retrieval system, or transmitted,
in any form or by any means, electronic,
mechanical, recording or otherwise
without prior permission of the publishers.

Also by Ian Carter:
The Red Kite (2001; 2nd edition 2007)
The Red Kite's Year (2019)
Human, Nature (2021)
Rhythms of Nature (2022)
The Hen Harrier's Year (2022)

Printed in the UK by Halstan

To Hazel, with enduring thanks. You were, of course, a big part of *Human, Nature* and *Rhythms of Nature*, but this book wouldn't have happened without you.

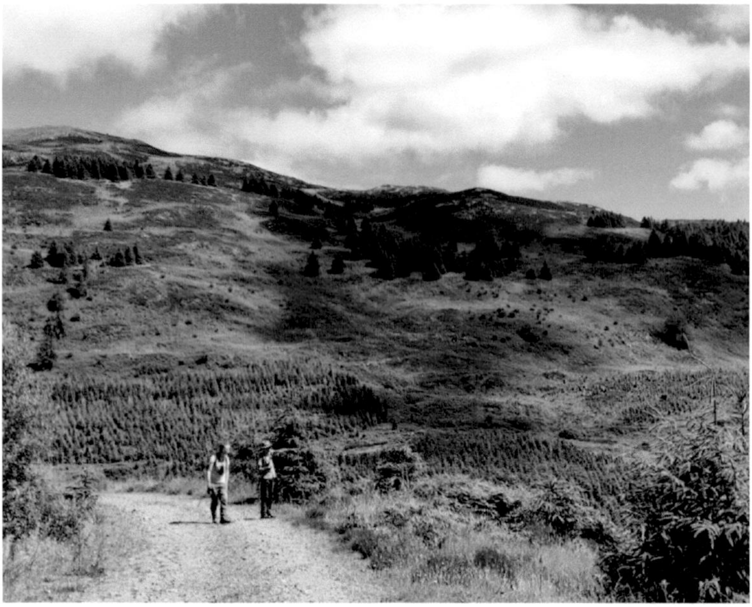

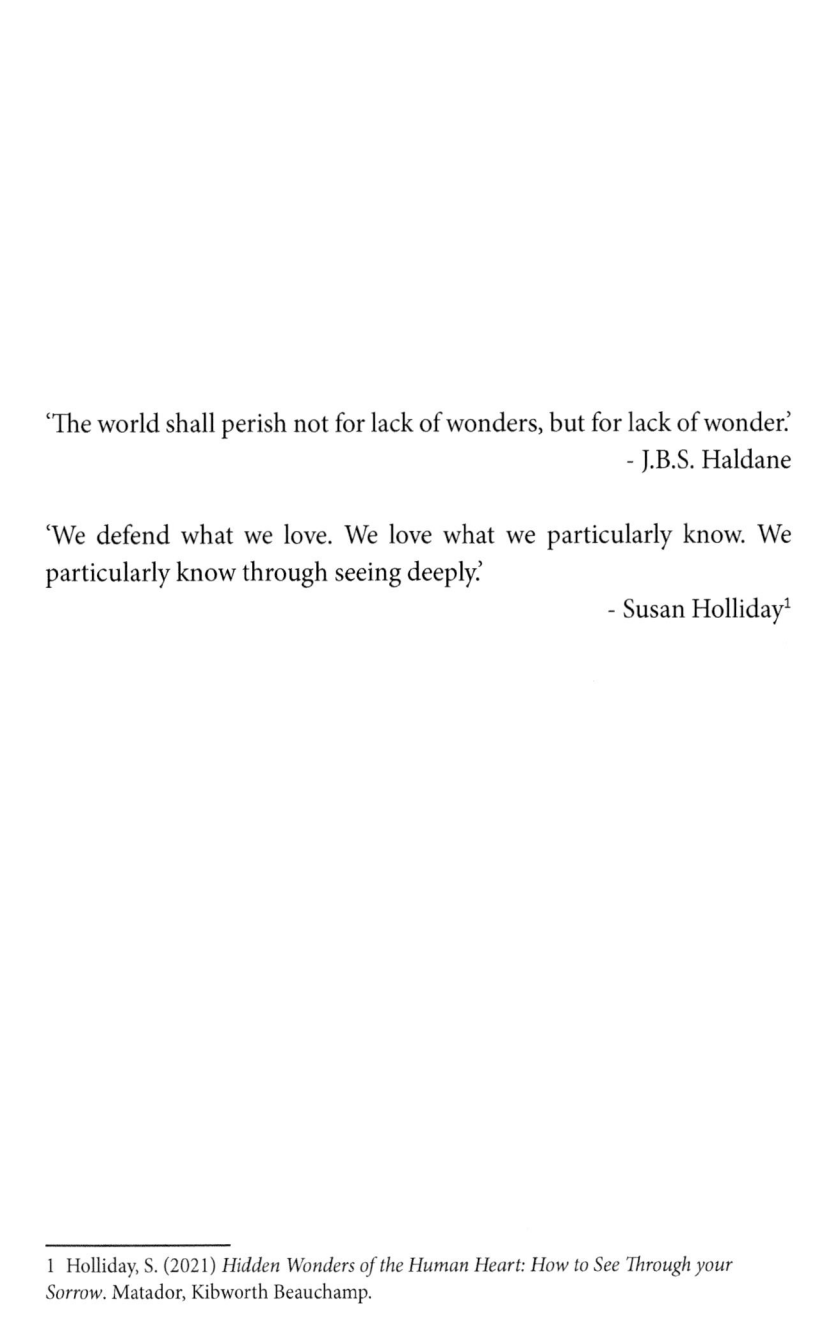

'The world shall perish not for lack of wonders, but for lack of wonder.'
- J.B.S. Haldane

'We defend what we love. We love what we particularly know. We particularly know through seeing deeply.'
- Susan Holliday[1]

---

1 Holliday, S. (2021) *Hidden Wonders of the Human Heart: How to See Through your Sorrow*. Matador, Kibworth Beauchamp.

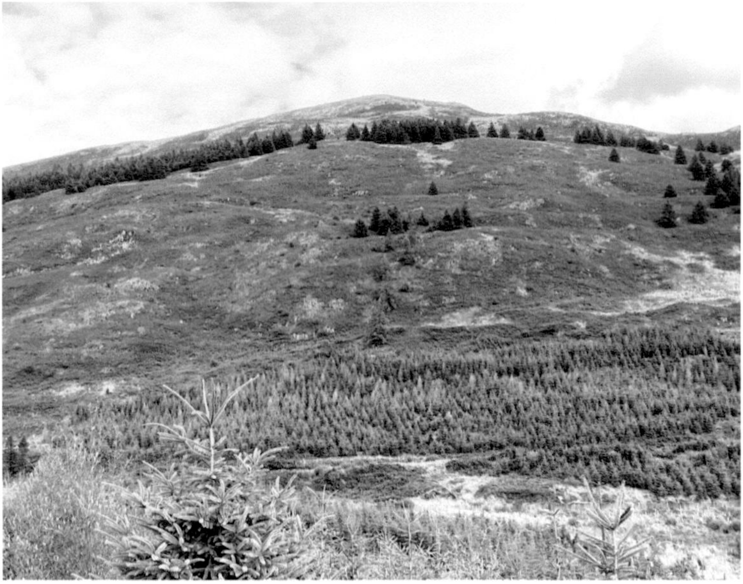

Contents

	Acknowledgements	xi
1	Heading north	1
2	A guiding spirit	11
3	Layers in the landscape	21
4	Squirrel wars – life on the front line	31
5	Wildness on the farm	39
6	Wildness in the hills	51
7	The new wild	61
8	The land's edge	73
9	Island life	91
10	House-sharing	105
11	The high tops	115
12	The eagle's way	121
13	A million stones	129
14	A watering hole in the hills	135
15	The wildwood	143
16	Wildwater	151
17	Time well spent	159
18	End notes	169
	The wildlife	175

Acknowledgements

Writing is a solitary occupation, especially when it's for a book about wandering the local countryside, usually alone. So I've appreciated the recent shared wildlife experiences here, and occasionally further afield, with Hazel, Ali, Ben, Brian and Margaret Carter; Gavin and Cliona Dando; Jackie, Jon, Danny and Katie Harris, Stephen Rutt (thank you for the waxwings) and Alick Simmons.

We are lucky to have neighbours who share our interest in wildlife and send us updates and photos of what they've seen in their part of the glen. I'm grateful to Janet and Brian Hamilton (and very jealous of their garden leverets and barn owls), Graham and Louise Roger, and Craig, Louis and Ann Marshall and family down at the farm. Thanks, Louis, for making sure we still had water after that brutal cold spell last December. I hope you can forgive my inexpert digressions into farming and the way that wildlife responds. Modern farming will always have some downsides, as well as benefits, for nature, but it is a privilege to live in a place where the wildlife remains so rich and diverse. June Nelson kindly visited us to talk about wildlife past and present at our new home, where she had lived with her late husband Bryan for over 20 years.

John Lind and Mia Misso from the Solway Forests Red Squirrel Network, and Kat Walsh at Natural England provided invaluable advice about red squirrels and the pox disease that afflicts them. Liam Wilson at The Royal (Dick) School of Veterinary Studies, University of Edinburgh, provided helpful guidance based on a photograph of a sick squirrel that had been visiting the garden. The Dunmuir Veterinary Group in Castle Douglas took delivery of a dead squirrel so that it could be sent for a specialist post-mortem.

The National Trust for Scotland staff at Threave House provided useful information about the wildlife on their nature reserve, including breeding ospreys, helping to confirm that their birds are probably the ones that visit us occasionally.

I bumped into Sue Gilroy as she was doing her weekly check of the sheep on Hestan Island, and she was kind enough to stop and explain some of the fascinating history of the island and its wildlife. She suggested that I look out for one special animal while on the island. I did just that, and later that evening it paid rich dividends. More about that in Chapter 9, Island life.

Social media has its limitations and downsides. But Nature Twitter is an enduringly helpful and friendly place. I'm grateful to various people who provided useful information, identified tricky (and some not-so-tricky) plants, fungi and invertebrates from my photographs, or took part in discussions relevant to the topics I've written about here: Nick Acheson, Philip Amies, Mark Avery, Amy-Jane Beer, Richard Broughton, Alan Brown, Daniel Buckley, Paul Cantwell, Nicola Chester, Kerrie Ann Gardner, James Gilbert, Tim Hannigan, Brigit Strawbridge Howard, Steve Jones, Dawn Lawrence, Alex Lees, Chantal Lyons, Ollie Metcalf, Jon Moses, Moira O'Donnell, Clare Pinches, Stephen Rutt, Guy Shorrock, Craig Shuttleworth, Richard Smyth, Alick Simmons, Alan Stewart, Ian Tattum, Ruth Tingay, Paul Tout, Kevin Walker, Hugh Webster, Rob Williams and Sophie Yeo. I will, I'm sure, have missed a few people, so my apologies for that.

It was a real pleasure to work with the dedicated team at Whittles, always on hand to provide advice and guidance when needed: thanks to Juliette Currums, Kerrie Moncur, Kerry O'Keefe, Sue Steven and Keith Whittles. A special thank you to copy editor Caroline Petherick. She took great care with the manuscript, hunting down errors and inconsistencies, and adding insight, understanding and often humour to her notes, some of which have found their way into the book. Revising a text handled with such sensitivity and perception was a rare pleasure.

I'm grateful to Karen Menarry, whose artwork graces the cover. To find such an evocative image of the very glen I'd been writing about hanging on a shop wall in Castle Douglas was a moment of good fortune I will long remember. Now we have several of her beautiful prints hanging on our own walls.

Acknowledgements

The photographs are my own with one exception. For that, I'm very grateful to Cliona Dando, who managed to catch me and her husband Gavin off guard and so provided the only image in the book to include humans.

Hazel Carter read through an initial draft of the book, scribbling things like 'sounds dull' and 'muddled and confused' in the margins. She has (I hope) spared you from these twin horrors.

I mustn't forget Teazel, our hopelessly untrainable cocker spaniel with an irrepressible knack for attracting wildlife and finding her way onto the page. For 13 years she got me out into the countryside every day, even when I wasn't much in the mood. Even in old age she worked her way into the story, though this turned out to be her final book.

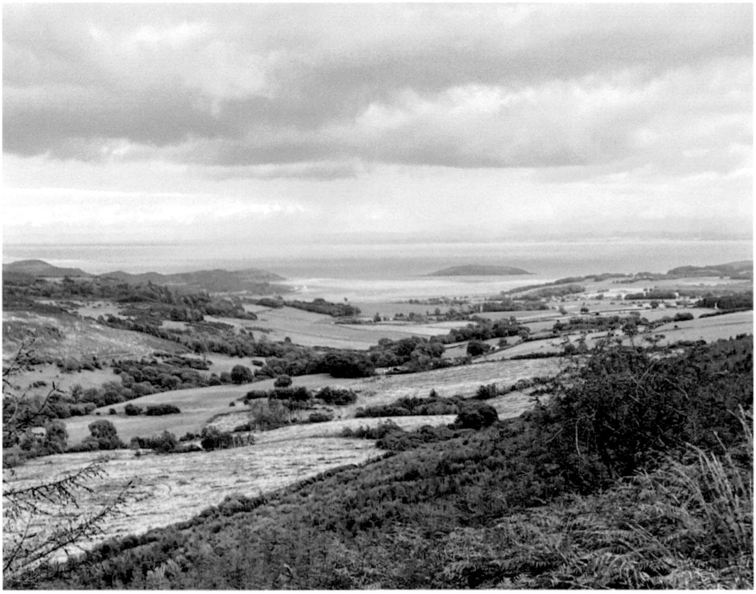

1

Heading north

Leaving the south-west of England for a wilder landscape.

We lived in a rented house on a dairy farm in mid-Devon for five years. Having retired early, I had more time to indulge my interest in wildlife, and it was with that in mind that we had moved to Devon. After a quarter of a century in the flatlands of the Cambridgeshire Fens, mid-Devon offered a refreshing change of scene. It's a wilder landscape than the Fens, although it too is dominated by intensive agriculture. Here, though, it is still possible to find lost corners where natural vegetation predominates and human influence is minimal. There are streams that wind through waterlogged, uncultivated ground, moors that have escaped the plough, and forgotten fragments of woodland left largely undisturbed for decades.[2]

And yet, despite the attractions, I found myself increasingly ill at ease. Our regular trips to the west coast of Scotland were part of the problem. They offered a reminder that wild landscapes on a bigger, more impressive scale still exist, even here in Britain. The human condition, it seems, is always to strive for more. That usually means more money or a better job. For me, however, what keeps pushing itself to the fore is the desire to live in ever wilder places. Having put up with the dull uniformity of the Fens for 25 years, I felt that mid-Devon was a step in the right direction. But still, after five years, there was something missing.

I was pondering these things one weekend, early in November. I'd gone out into the garden with half an hour to kill before the football

---

[2] Our time in mid-Devon is described in Carter, I. (2022) *Rhythms of Nature: Wildlife and Wild Places Between the Moors*. Pelagic Publishing, Exeter.

started. My intention was to pull a few weeds from the patio, but the pair of stonechats that had been with us the past few days provided a welcome distraction. They were using the wreckage of docks, thistles and dead hogweed in the most overgrown part of the garden; launching aerial sorties from the top of the stems, in between dodging the garden's resident robins, incensed at the unexpected competition.

Cars were passing on the road to the next village. The dull thump of a distant gas gun was another artificial addition to the soundscape. This gas gun, I knew by now, pumped out two little explosions, a few seconds apart, every 30 minutes. You get used to these intrusions, I suppose. If you live near a road, cars are not something you can afford to get too worked up about. And wherever there is agriculture, birds must be dissuaded from the fields. We put up with these things because we have no real choice.

And yet, surely, I did have a choice.

A late red admiral floated by, flicking powerful wings seemingly at random, oblivious to existential worries. It came to rest on one of the patio slabs to soak up the last of the afternoon's sun. As I watched it, the gas gun sounded again, and I knew that half an hour must have passed; the football would be kicking off and the weeds were safe for another day. As closely as I can pinpoint it, that was the moment my mind was made up.

* * *

We've made the drive from the south of England to the Scottish Highlands many times. The relentless push up the M6; the packed, multi-lane flyovers through Glasgow; heading north along the beautiful tree-lined roads around Loch Lomond, and then up and away into the mountains. Once past Carlisle, though, few people think to turn left before Glasgow. We've done so twice: firstly on a house-hunting trip, and then to move in.

Our move here was a classic British compromise. I'm no longer tied to a particular location, but my wife Hazel still works for Natural England, and while they are a creditably flexible employer, they like their staff to reside within striking distance of the relevant country, if not actually within its borders. Then there was family to think about; we didn't want to put too much distance between ourselves and our loved ones. We were hindered by the global pandemic and a housing market that chose just the wrong moment to go into overdrive, but eventually we found somewhere. The house is on its own, on a farm track that runs up the glen into the hills above the village of Auchencairn. It's a little over an hour's drive to the border with England; on a clear day Hazel can at least see into the land of her employer. The silver waters of the Solway Firth form a pale band away to the south, beyond which are the peaks of the Lake District, topped with snow through the colder months.

I have said it's a compromise. Without the constraints we might have sought out a more remote location, in the Highlands, perhaps, or one of the islands. But if the local landscape doesn't have quite the same feel as the Highlands and Islands further north, it does have its own special appeal. In mid-Devon it's difficult to put a few hundred metres between yourself and the nearest house or road. You are rarely far from a fence-line or a flowerless field of rye grass, and the fragments of good wildlife habitat are just that – fragments – in a landscape dominated by humans. In our part of Galloway, more of the land is self-willed, or at least less constrained by human activities. And it's on a different scale. Making an escape into a world where wildlife takes centre stage is no more difficult than stepping over the garden fence and disappearing into the hills. Forty-five minutes from the house I can be tucked away in a place where no artificial sounds permeate, there is no one else around, and there are no roads or buildings to snag the eye.

When we first viewed our new home, red kites cruised overhead and siskins swarmed over the birdfeeders. A semi-tame red squirrel sat casually by the patio window, nibbling a peanut, tail wrapped over its back for warmth, while the estate agent waxed lyrical about local amenities. We were no longer listening to him – but no matter; the sale had been made.

* * *

It is mid-morning and I'm sitting on a low rocky outcrop on the southern flank of Bengairn, legs dangling into the dense, leggy heather below. It has taken me an hour of brisk walking, mostly over uneven ground, mostly uphill, to get here. The house is an insignificant pale smudge down in the glen below.[3] My leg muscles are burning, and I've earned the right to pause a while, to survey the scene and reflect on all that I've come to love about this place. This is a favourite spot. From here, the glen stretches away from the hill country down to the village 3 miles away and, just beyond that, the northern shore of the Solway.

I can reach the coast in under an hour's walk from home, across gentler terrain that is easier on the legs. A rough track heads south, passing through the farmyard at Auchenleck, and joining a narrow lane that runs into the village perched above the bay. If I have the whole day, I can continue to the towering, convoluted seabird cliffs that start at Balcary Point, looking out over the low green dome of Hestan Island, guarding the entrance to the bay.

Before we moved into our house, we were surprised to learn from the previous owners that the renowned ornithologist and gannet expert Bryan Nelson had once lived in it. While here he edited a small guidebook highlighting the best places for watching birds in Galloway. This is how it starts:[4]

> Galloway is varied, beautiful and rich in bird-life. Within its boundaries, mountain and moor march with loch, woodland and river and many a farm is blessed with those wild corners that are so valuable to flowers, insects, amphibia, reptiles, birds and mammals. Rich estuaries are flanked by rugged coastline and there are uninhabited offshore islands. Whilst much of Britain

---

3 Having lived south of the border for most of my life it feels almost fraudulent to adopt words like 'glen', 'burn', 'merse' and 'dyke' instead of 'valley', 'stream', 'marsh' and 'wall' in this book. It's as if I'm trying too hard to demonstrate an understanding and connection that isn't quite there yet. I wouldn't use these terms in casual conversation (not yet) and that's not really how I think of them. In my head I'm wading a *stream* or hopping over a stone *wall*. But would a Scottish writer living in Devon use 'glen' and 'burn', and if they did would it not jar a little? The little watercourse that flows below the house is marked on the Ordnance Survey map as the Hass Burn. Who am I to change it?

4 Nelson, B. (ed.) (1989) *Bird Walks in Dumfries & Galloway: 32 Scenic, Bird-rich Walks & Locations by Galloway Birdwatchers.* The Galloway RSPB Members Group, Newton Stewart.

lives with increasing apprehension among the ravages caused by industry, large-scale monoculture farming and the pathetically short-sighted destruction of lovely countryside, Galloway is still a microcosm of all that is bonny in Scotland.

Galloway has not been spared from damaging developments and the impacts of intensive farming and forestry. It has seen plenty of the 'short-sighted destruction of lovely countryside' that has visited the rest of Britain. And yet Bryan's upbeat assessment, made a quarter of a century ago, is, I think, still broadly true today. I took something else from Bryan's introduction. Although he was writing about Galloway as a whole, his words – almost every one of them – equally well describe the immediate surroundings of his, and now our, home.

There is, then, something special about this glen, aside from the pleasant views and the delightfully varied wildlife: *this place is wild Galloway in miniature.* Within walking distance of the house is the coast with its mudflats, merse and rough grazing, frequented by waders and, in winter, noisy flocks of pink-footed and barnacle geese. There are the cliffs that, come spring, fill with kittiwakes, fulmars, guillemots and razorbills. The land around the house is mostly farmed, and some of it is worked intensively, grazed hard by livestock, or cut for silage several times each summer. Here, wildlife is largely pushed aside. But there are rougher patches too. Fields littered with rocky outcrops or prone to waterlogging are managed with a lighter touch. Wild flowers get a chance to flourish, gorse springs up in dense patches, and invertebrates fly up or scuttle out of the way as you walk. Here, there are things for birds to eat and places for them to nest.

The higher ground, above the stone dykes of the farm, is a mix of the two habitats that cover so much of Galloway's hill country. There is open moorland, cloaked with heather and bracken where the land is well drained, with sphagnum moss, cottongrass and the yellow spikes of bog asphodel in the wetter places. Then there are the plantations. They are mostly of Sitka spruce, a tree brought here from the west coast of North America, in blocks of different ages depending on how long ago they were planted. There are also small plantings of native deciduous trees – a token gesture, perhaps, in a place swamped with alien conifers, but welcome nonetheless.

There are other features too, including a small loch on the edge of the hills and several more on the lower ground, closer to the sea, fringed with reeds, bulrushes and willow scrub. There are ponds up in the hills, perhaps created by foresters to provide a water source in case of fire. Arable fields, and the birds that use them, are in short supply, but there is a handful of fields where fodder crops are grown for the livestock. Best of all, along the burn that runs down through the glen, just below the house, the ground is rocky, uneven and prone to flooding. Here, patches of deciduous woodland have survived, and I can slip away into another world. Ancient ash trees tower overhead, red squirrels skip through the hazels, and brown trout seek out quieter pools. In May, the woodland floor is a haze of blue.

All this is shoehorned into our little corner of Galloway. Add in the village, and a sprinkling of farms and houses, together with their gardens, and this glen is indeed a microcosm of all that Galloway has to offer. At the same time, then, this book is a portrait of the varied wildlife that scrapes a living from a singular patch of ground, and, by default, an exploration of the wide range of wildlife that anyone visiting Galloway can expect to encounter if time is spent in the right habitats.

* * *

Our home, Mine House, was built roughly two centuries ago for the manager of a small ironstone mine that lies one field away, long since reclaimed by woodland. It is one of just three houses in the upper part of the glen, strung out along the farm track. Looking north, there is nothing but fields and hills. A walk in that direction takes in Bengairn and Screel Hill, though there is no path. It takes two hours, hopping the odd stone dyke and pushing through deep heather, to re-find civilisation: a single-track lane that runs up to the village of Gelston.

My family, I think, see this choice of home (and the other isolated houses before it) as an intolerance for fellow humans, an attempt to withdraw, even. There's a little of that, I suppose. More, though, it's because in a place with few people, wildlife takes on a greater significance. Sights and sounds are dominated by creatures other than ourselves. Connections become deeper. It is, then, not so much withdrawal *from* people as a gravitation *towards* the more-than-human world; something that is an indispensable part of my life.

Of course, even here the influence of people is imprinted boldly onto the land. A book about wildlife must also deal with the way that humanity interacts with everything else in the natural world. Galloway has a wild feel to it, certainly, but here in Britain no true wilderness remains. Humans have influenced this glen, and the wider area, for thousands of years. And the pace of change has picked up in modern times, with consequences that are all too obvious.

Animals that once benefitted from wide expanses of open moorland and rough grassland have not fared well. The habitats they rely on have been diminished, either smothered with a blanket of conifers, or 'improved', to create bland, heavily managed grassland. Birds that try to nest on the remaining moors must now contend with abundant predators that take refuge in the forests. On the lower ground new agricultural machines and the intensity of grazing make it difficult for birds to rear their young. We see curlews in winter, foraging languidly along the shoreline with their outsize down-curved bills. Occasionally they fly up to the fields near the house to feed, swapping lugworms for earthworms. But come the spring the haunting cries of a once common breeding bird are no longer heard. The local fields would once have held breeding snipe, and lapwings, and corncrakes, but no more. Even the humble skylark, a formerly abundant bird, familiar to all, has retreated into the hills.

The losses are stark. That we are not more shocked by them is because they happen gradually. Numbers decline a little, year on year. Species that were once abundant become a little less so. Animals that are already scarce become ever harder to find. Then they are seen so rarely that when they finally fade out completely we barely notice. We get used to things the way they are, and forget (or have never experienced) the way they once were. In the end, we make do with what is left because, well … what else can we do?

Not all is doom and gloom. Some animals have the happy knack of adapting well to highly modified landscapes, while others have benefitted from our changing attitudes. Wild geese make a good living from grazing the coastal grasslands; their numbers are on the up. The spreading of cattle slurry as fertiliser gives grass a competitive edge over once common wild flowers. But the rich crop of grass is food for the geese, and the fields also ensure a plentiful supply of earthworms that are forced up to the surface by the slurry. Foxes, badgers, birds of prey and gulls take full advantage.

Red kites, buzzards and eagles all once suffered because of our intolerance for anything that might compete with us for food or threaten our sport. Now they are coming back, the kites and eagles with a helping hand from conservationists. The lithe, inquisitive animal that one evening elicited involuntary gasps and cries of 'wow!' as it skipped up the steps to our patio was evidence enough that pine martens, too, are on their way back. This falls far short of making up for all that has been lost, and the returning predators can make life even more difficult for vulnerable species, but we cling desperately to these gains, and to the knowledge that relentless decline and loss is not the only possible narrative.

* * *

I have tried to write the sort of book that I always look for but rarely find when I move to a new area or visit somewhere different. Not a wildlife guidebook as such, although it serves a loosely similar purpose, and certainly not a survey of the region's best sites for wildlife. Rather, this is a description of the wildlife that is typically encountered in this part of Britain; the things I've come across when wandering through the varied habitats of this glen – the things that you too might expect to find in your own wanderings if you spend time in similar places. At the end of the book is a list of all the birds (and other vertebrates) I've seen, with brief notes about them.

The book has something else I look for in the writing of others: a sense of the human response to wildlife. Some people enjoy wild geese for the 'sport' they provide, while for others the pleasure is in the watching. Not everyone would wish to share their home, as we do, with hundreds of pipistrelle bats. I know people who fence out the local badgers from their garden rather than tempting them in with food. We are all very different. Another person living in the same house and walking the same landscape would write a very different book.

I now spend more time outdoors than at any point since childhood. In those distant, hazy days, it was routine to hop the garden wall and head off into the surrounding countryside. 'Be back in time for tea' was the only rule. Five decades later I do much the same thing. The enlightened Scottish access legislation helps. When we lived in Devon there was the constant fear of challenge whenever I presumed to stray from the path. Here I can wander, anxiety-free, in any direction. I don't need to ask the local landowners whether that's okay. It *is* okay.

Despite all that we hear about the perilous state of the world, there is a joy in watching wildlife, whether that's red squirrels nibbling hazelnuts a few inches from the window, or a golden eagle cruising along the ridgeline half a mile away. The benefits to human health of spending time in nature are increasingly well understood. We know this intuitively. Now scientists are beginning to unpick the mechanisms. They are starting to show that we *feel* better when we pay attention to the wildlife that lives all around us for one simple reason: we *are* better. Every time I close the back door behind me and head out into the glen I am reminded of this truth.

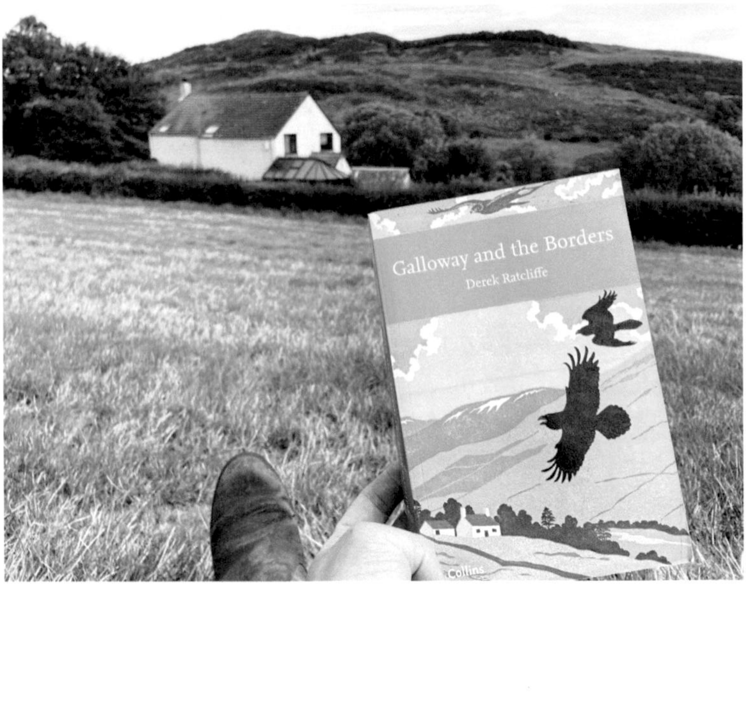

Galloway and the Borders
Derek Ratcliffe
Collins

2

A guiding spirit

Exploring the glen with a conservation hero, and reconnecting with red kites.

Our move to Galloway unexpectedly reacquainted me with someone I've always looked up to. Soon after we arrived I was searching for books about the area, and came across Derek Ratcliffe's *Galloway and the Borders* in the renowned New Naturalist series.[5] I couldn't believe I'd overlooked it, especially as I own every other book that he has written. The omission was quickly put right. The book – the last Derek would write – has a pair of Robert Gillmor's characteristic ravens on the cover. They are flying over an isolated white house with a slate roof. A small burn runs through the glen below, flanked by low, rounded hills. They might as well be our local ravens, our white house with its slate roof, our burn and our hills.

I joined the old Nature Conservancy Council (NCC) in 1990. It was my first full-time job in conservation. I didn't know it at the time, but Derek Ratcliffe had retired just a year earlier, after 15 years as its chief scientist. He had left during a turbulent period, just before the NCC was divided into separate bodies covering England, Wales and Scotland. The split was widely seen as an attempt by politicians to weaken the organisation, punishment for speaking out about one of the most contentious conservation issues of the day: the loss of irreplaceable peatlands in the flow country of Caithness and Sutherland through ploughing, draining and the planting of non-native conifers, encouraged by tax breaks for wealthy speculators.

---

5 Ratcliffe, D. (2007) *Galloway and the Borders.* Collins, London.

I met Derek face to face only once. As it happens, it was in southern Scotland in 2003, at a conference about birds of prey. We were introduced by a mutual friend. I don't recall the conversation, but I imagine it was slightly awkward, of the kind that takes place when two people who are not good at small talk find themselves having to try. I may have updated him on progress with the Red Kite Reintroduction Project. It would have been the only subject of interest to us both about which I could have told him something he didn't already know.

In later years, I got to know him – or so it felt – through his books. Again and again, he proved the point that time spent outdoors (often in the hills, often alone) was time well spent. He was drawn to places where wildlife was free-willed, with sufficient distance from human infrastructure and activities to express itself. Whether the book was about ravens, peregrines, the Lake District, mountains in general, or – as I am now finding out – Galloway and the Borders, his passion for the uplands was obvious.

In the end, Derek's knowledge and love for these places became a double-edged sword. With greater knowledge comes easier recognition of the devastation we have wrought. In desperation, later in life he began to make annual trips to Lapland – and, of course, wrote another excellent book based on his visits. As he made clear: 'Probably [these trips] are a form of escapism, when I leave the awful problems of UK conservation behind, as well as the gruesome events of the world in general.'[6]

One of the 'awful problems' in the UK was the blanketing of vast areas of the uplands with monocultures of planted, non-native conifers. In *Galloway and the Borders*, while Derek retains his typical balanced and scientific approach, he is scathing about the new plantations and the resulting losses of wildlife. He was uniquely well placed to comment; he witnessed their march across the landscape at first hand on his annual visits to Galloway. His book includes poignant photographs that he had taken as a young adult when first

---

[6] Marren, P. (2015) 'Derek and I: A correspondence.' In *Nature's Conscience: The Life and Legacy of Derek Ratcliffe*. Edited by Thompson, D., Birks, H. and Birks, J. Langford Press, Kings Lynn.

wandering these hills in the 1940s and 1950s to seek out their rare plants and birds. These are paired with his more recent pictures, taken decades later. Here are the very same places, now smothered under a blanket of dark green – stark, straight-lined edges scarring the hills. He describes the impacts in detail, setting out the losses as well as the limited gains of adaptable species that have moved into the new forests. Ultimately, though, it was the loss of the overall character of the landscape that hit him hardest. He suggests that time spent walking in the hills is the only way to fully appreciate what has happened, and he offers a hint that not all conservationists will fully share his strong feelings:

> You have to go and walk among them [the forests] and weigh it all up for yourself. No doubt some will feel that, on balance, the trees are a worthwhile addition to scenery and habitat, and will have no sense of what has been lost. Maybe some will welcome the tracks that give ready access to country once accessible only by hard walking, but enthusiasts for wilderness will find it now greatly reduced in extent.

In our old Devon haunts there wasn't much point getting worked up about the prevalence of roads or endless bright green monocultures of grass. But here in Galloway, I soon realised that I would have to make my peace with the plantations. I now have plenty of time to walk among them and weigh it all up for myself, as Derek suggests. Even the outlook from the house invites reflection. Siskins on the feeders and red squirrels squabbling over peanuts help make a case for the plantations; both have benefitted from the increase in conifers. But the dark, looming shapes on the hills scream of interference and artificiality. It's a subject I'll return to later in the book.

* * *

A lunchtime dog walk to the boundary dyke between the farm and the hill country above. I'm trying to clear my head after *another* morning unpacking boxes. It's early March, and in the absence of much in the way of wildlife activity I find my mind drifting. I'm thinking of a paper someone sent me suggesting that the hills near Auchencairn – the hills here – may have held the last population of lynx in Britain before they finally became extinct. A plausible account was provided in 1760 by a traveller, one Richard Pococke, over 1,000 years after the date they were previously believed to have disappeared:[7]

> They have also a wild cat three times as big as the common cat …. They are of a yellow red colour, their breasts and sides white. They take fowls and lambs, & breed two at a time … ; and it is said they will attack a man who would attempt to take their young ones.

The lynx is a staggeringly elusive animal. Elsewhere in Europe it's possible to spend a lifetime in areas where they are present without ever catching a glimpse of one. Could they have clung on here, even beyond 1760? Might they still be here now? I know it's impossible. But I keep half an eye out anyway.

We may yet get our lynx back through reintroduction. The red kites that grace the local countryside show what can be done. I'd missed seeing this bird regularly during our time in Devon – but here, thanks to a release project in Galloway in the early 2000s, they are a near-daily presence. Today, the hole-digging exploits of our ageing cocker spaniel result in an especially close encounter. I first notice the kite on the far side of the glen and watch as it drifts across towards us to take a closer look, wings flexing rather than flapping as it works the breeze. Some seabirds, albatrosses for example, have such efficient flight that they apparently burn more energy when sitting on the cold sea than they do in the air. I suspect that in a favourable wind the kite, too, with its light frame, long wings and long, flexing tail, wastes precious little energy as it sweeps above the land.

---

[7] Raye, L. (2021) 'An 18th-century reference to a Eurasian lynx (*Lynx lynx*) in Scotland.' *Mammal Communications* 7: 47–52. For an accessible summary (and much else besides) see also Raye, L. (2023) *The Atlas of Early Modern Wildlife: Britain and Ireland between the Middle Ages and the Industrial Revolution.* Pelagic Publishing, London.

A guiding spirit

The bird loses height and circles low over the dog a few times, now flapping its wings to hold position. It is assessing what feeding opportunities there might be: is that dog down there feeding on an animal carcass, perhaps? Finding nothing of the sort, it floats away on the breeze to continue its never-ending search for food. For most modern humans these days, the next meal is a forgone conclusion. But wild animals don't live that way. Every day begins with an urgent quest: find enough to eat to be able to keep going, or the adventure comes to an end.

The nature of this particular encounter sheds light on the red kite's turbulent history in Britain. Its insatiable curiosity and lack of fear of humans were once a recipe for disaster, making it an easy bird to kill, and hastening its demise. Now, in more enlightened times, its inquisitive behaviour serves it well. The reintroduced kites take advantage of food provided by humans, including at feeding stations, refuse tips and even in gardens. The bird's endless curiosity and a lack of fear have become (by and large) a help, not a hindrance.

Derek's book, published in 2007, records the tentative early stages of the kite's return. At the time, following the release of 104 young birds, there were just nine breeding pairs in Galloway. I played the smallest of parts in this project, little suspecting that 20 years later I'd be living here, able to watch the birds every day. As part of my work with red kites in England I helped transfer to Galloway a batch of young kites collected from nests in the Chiltern Hills. I drove north from there to rendezvous with the project officer, Kevin Duffy, at a service station somewhere along the A1 in northern England, and we transferred the birds to his vehicle so they could complete their journey. Now, when I watch a kite, I sometimes wonder if it's possible, just possible, it might be one of the youngsters that I transported. It's a long shot. But recently a bird released in the Chilterns in 1994 was taken into care not too far away from the release site. It was almost 29 years old.

There are well over 150 pairs of red kites in Galloway, and the bird is once again a reassuring, established presence. It is a delight to watch. And it fits this landscape so well that it scarcely seems possible it was gone for so long.

During these early decades of the 21st century other predators and scavengers have done well locally. Ravens are less heavily persecuted than they once were, although they still occasionally cause problems for sheep farmers in the lambing season. Peregrines too have made a comeback following the devastating losses caused by organochlorine pesticides in the 1960s, a problem that first came to light because of Derek's studies. He was especially fond of both these birds, and as a young adult spent hours tramping through Galloway's hill country, seeking out their nest sites. He later wrote the definitive monograph for each of them.[8] He would have been delighted to see them thriving now, after all their problems.

We see ravens often enough, usually alerted by their distinctive 'gronking' calls as they pass high overhead. I'm drawn to watching them more than any other bird, for no other reason than to find out what they will do next; they rarely disappoint. One of their best tricks is to flip over onto their back for a few seconds before righting themselves. Sometimes they appear to pull off a remarkable 360-degree roll, though it's difficult to be sure it's not an illusion as it happens so quickly; have they really spun through the full circle, or do they just flip back into position so quickly that the human eye is fooled? Consulting Derek's raven book, I encounter his typical scientific caution; he is unconvinced, despite the apparently reliable reports of several observers. He also notes that the functional significance of this rolling-over display is not entirely clear. That's fine with me. An air of mystery only adds to the bird's appeal.

I can mimic a raven's call (if I'm sure there's no one within earshot), and sometimes it's good enough to fool the real thing for a few short, life-enhancing seconds. The 'victim' loses height and circles around to take a closer look before realising it's been had, sometimes firing off a disgruntled 'gronk' of rebuke before continuing on its way.

I see peregrines far less often, but soon after we moved here I watched a pair performing aerobatics around a rocky crag on the far side of the glen. As I walked across the sheep field below, both birds were hanging in the air, sweeping from side to side and then diving

---

8 Ratcliffe, D. (1997) *The Raven*. Poyser, London; Ratcliffe, D. (1993) *The Peregrine* (second edition). Poyser, London.

down on folded wings towards the ground. Later, I could see one of the pair standing on a ledge that looked promising as a potential nest site. Back at the house I set up the telescope and peered hopefully at the ledge but there was no further activity. I suspect they were just feeling this place out. In the end they must have moved deeper into the hills to a more secluded location.

Another animal to have made a comeback is the pine marten. I was surprised to find that this most enigmatic of mammals receives just a few lines in Derek's Galloway book. He observes that it had been lost due to persecution by around 1850, and mentions a fledgling reintroduction project in the Galloway Forest Park, led by the Forestry Commission. Noting the initial signs of success, he remarks, somewhat dryly, that 'the view that modern Galloway forests can support the Pine Marten thus appears to be upheld'. Evidently there had been some debate about the matter. Derek's lack of enthusiasm is, I suspect, because he believed success for the project would be a feather in the cap (and another selling point) for the plantations.

A few years on and any lingering doubts about the suitability of the landscape have been banished. Pine martens are now widespread across the area due to a combination of releases, the installation of boxes to encourage breeding, and natural spread. Much like the kite, it is an adaptable and resilient animal, able to thrive in our modern landscapes if only it is left alone. The animal that skipped onto our patio early one evening to filch peanuts is evidence enough of that.

* * *

Derek was as good an all-round naturalist as you'll find. He was especially knowledgeable about birds and plants, and an expert on some of the most difficult and underappreciated plant groups, including ferns, mosses and liverworts. Birders tend to look up most of the time, while botanists keep their heads bowed, scanning the ground ahead. Derek presumably alternated between the two. And when looking down in Galloway he regularly came across an animal I hoped I'd find here. One of the reasons for my optimism is Derek's book. He writes that it is 'more numerous in the Galloway hills than in any other uplands I have visited in Britain'. It appears that it was not popular with the local farmers, who 'killed them widely' and even tolerated the wild goats 'because of their reputation for killing [them] by trampling on them'. Foresters, too, disliked them, and in the days before legal protection (and, you suspect, for a while afterwards) 'large numbers were killed by the men planting the young trees, who regard them as a constant hazard in their daily work'. Derek had his own words of caution: 'They are fond of basking on rocks, ledges and banks ... and it is as well to watch where you put your hands.'

I am indeed watching where I put my hands when I find my first Galloway adder, on the hillside overlooking the house on an unseasonably warm day towards the end of March. It's a young animal born last summer, just 18–20 centimetres long and not much thicker than a pencil. It has pulled itself up onto a rock to bask in the sun, but as I approach it does an about-turn before retreating slowly into a crevice. The south-facing slopes here, overlooking the house, look perfect for adders, with a mix of heather, bracken, bare ground and rocks for basking, and plenty of structure to provide hideouts where they can safely see out the winter. Now, whenever I scramble up these slopes I have Derek's warning in the back of my mind and I often reflect too on the unrivalled legacy he has left for today's naturalists and conservationists.

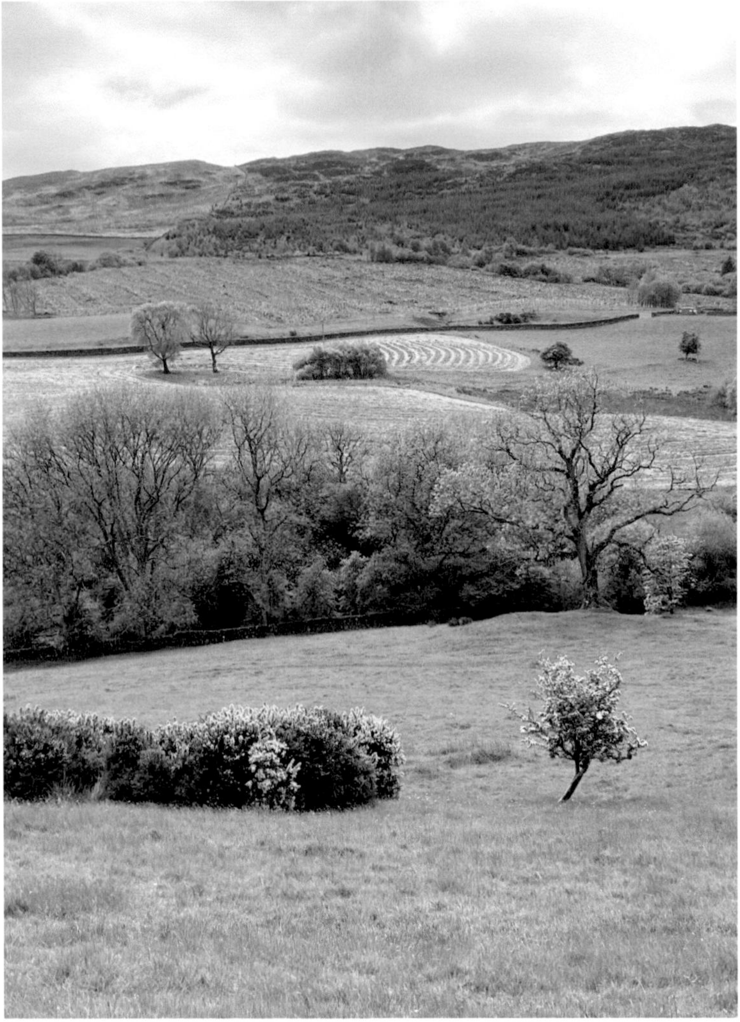

3

Layers in the landscape

Walking uphill through the glen's varied habitats, and walking back through time.

North of the house, a small, rocky burn runs through the wooded glen below. On the far side, the land opens out, sloping up and away to the stone cairn at the summit of Bengairn. It takes 90 minutes of hard climbing to reach the top. I've done this walk many times now, always taking a different route in the absence of a path or track, with the freedom to roam anywhere as a result of Scotland's far-sighted access legislation. The lack of a path is an invitation to nowhere or everywhere, depending on your mindset, but I love the autonomy that it brings. I walk here the way our dog walks: with intent and curiosity, but without a firm plan, and with only a rough idea of where to go next. My route is determined by events (birds mostly), the lie of the land and the moments when alternative options open up ahead and I pick one without really knowing why. 'I like the unpath best,' said a young child accompanying writer Nan Shepherd when pushing her way through leggy heather bushes in the Cairngorms.[9] She would have enjoyed Bengairn; it is all 'unpath'.

The glen is long but not especially wide. Walking up the slope towards Bengairn involves passing through a little slice of each of the broad habitat types that occur locally; the vegetation and the wildlife that uses it change as I pass from one to the next.

From the garden it's downhill initially, across the dullest of all the layers: a uniform, slurry-fed monoculture of grass. Then comes

---
9 The quote is from her classic book about walking in the Cairngorm mountains: Shepherd, N. (1977) *The Living Mountain*. Aberdeen University Press, Aberdeen.

the burn, fringed by woods of mature ash with hazel, downy birch, a few sessile and pedunculate oaks, and the occasional alder and wych elm. That's as easy as the walking gets; on the far side of the burn it's uphill all the way. First comes rough sheep pasture dotted with rocks, anthills and thickets of gorse. A stone dyke separates this from what lies above it. Climb over the dyke (at a place where wide, flat stepping-stones have been built into it) and you are standing at the edge of a huge area recently cleared of planted conifers. The colour palate changes instantly from the bright green of the pastures to the subdued yellows and browns of unfertilised grasses and bracken. This is the most structurally complex layer, with tangles of dead branches and stumps from the felled trees, drainage ditches and dense regrowth of brambles and other vegetation, responding to light after decades of darkness.

The next crop is already in the ground, so this place will change again in the coming years. The tiny trees are mostly Sitka spruce and Douglas fir, both from western North America, but a few native, deciduous trees have been planted around the edges.

Higher still is moorland that has escaped the planting. Here, it is less easy to make progress with patches of head-high bracken, and dense, leggy heather that tugs at your boots as you try to push through it. There are frequent outcrops of rock, which may have helped dissuade the foresters from venturing this far up the slope. The outcrops are free of vegetation, and often the easiest places to walk. The livestock are long gone from this area, kept out to protect the nearby forests, and in the absence of grazing this land feels wild; it has been subject to no obvious management by humans for several decades at least.

The final layer in the landscape is the open moorland towards the top of Bengairn. It lies above the dyke and is lightly grazed by sheep. The vegetation here is dominated by heather, which becomes lower and sparser as the altitude increases. There are a few scattered bushes and trees, established from berries dropped by birds or, in the case of the Sitka spruce, carried up on the wind from the forests below.

* * *

Wildlife responds to these layers of habitat in different ways. For some species the boundaries between them appear unimportant. These are the adaptable 'generalists', flexible in their approach to finding food and able to make a living almost anywhere.

The red kites and buzzards float above the garden, the top of the hill and everywhere in between. The badgers, foxes and roe deer, too, wander across the entirety of this landscape. Surprisingly to me, for an animal I associate with open country, brown hares do the same thing. My conception is based on spending years in the Cambridgeshire Fens where they frequent open country because there is often no other option. Here, however, I'm just as likely to see one in the ash woods, beneath the planted conifers or roaming across a clear-fell. Occasionally I disturb one hunkered down in one of our flowerbeds. Janet and Brian, who live in the house at the head of the valley, sent us photographs of two small leverets trailing their mother along the front drive, and then sheltering in the gap between a flowerpot and the wall of the house.

One morning, I was walking towards a hare on the farm track at the same time as a tractor, about 50 metres beyond it, was heading in our direction. The hare was standing side-on, each of its huge eyes facing towards a different approaching threat. *Shall I run first from the human or the tractor?* it must have been thinking – though who can imagine how it might process these two different images? In the end it ran a few metres towards me before jinking adeptly through a gap in the hedge and away across the field. Hazel once came across a lone hare on the rocky beach below the village. She was on the phone to a friend, and gave her an impromptu running commentary as the animal jumped off a low rock into the sea before swimming back to land, then running past her towards higher ground. A lot goes on behind those wild, all-seeing black-and-orange eyes.

The ubiquitous wren rivels the hare in its adaptability, one pair tucking a nest into the ivy on the back of the garage, while others sing from the piles of brash on the clear-fell, the root-plates of wind-blown spruce trees, or the heather shrubs up on the high tops. The robin, too, I see just outside the back door as well as on the hill slopes far above, wherever there are bushes for cover. It is a bird of contrasts, very tame or very wild, with a belligerent nature that belies its sweet song, placid appearance and undeserved reputation for adding tranquillity to a Christmas scene. When our dog is digging one of her futile holes, miles from civilisation, a robin will sometimes materialise and hop over to investigate. Back in the garden, we once watched *seven* together around the feeders in a spell of cold weather, the usual territorial animosity suspended (minor squabbles aside) in their desperation to access food. The robin is one of the last birds to be active at the end of each day, and there are even reports of them foraging by moonlight. They might take our garden handouts, but they are out there in the wild places too, still chasing invertebrates when human eyes are all but useless.

Other species are more discerning; I know I'll find them only in the layer of habitat that offers them what they need. The near-constant chattering of house sparrows becomes an absence as soon as I leave the house behind. Red squirrels are tied to the mature trees in the bottom of the glen – in the old woods or the garden. To find tree pipits I must head to the clear-fell. It's only here that I can hear their exuberant song as they launch themselves into the air, ending with a jubilant final flourish as they parachute back down to one of the old stumps or a pile of brash. In a few years, when the trees have grown up, they'll have moved on and I'll have to seek them out elsewhere. Most extreme of all is the dipper, a bird I only ever see along the narrow, winding line of the burn. Nowhere else will do.

* * *

Landscapes are layered in time as well as space. I can see this easily enough by looking at the old Ordnance Survey map of the area.[10] It was made in 1893 and while much is recognisable, there are some obvious differences too. The surrounding hills are open and unforested, and

---

10 These maps are the most beautiful, evocative things. Ours is from a series surveyed mainly in the second half of the 19th century. The scale is 25 inches to the mile, and the maps are black and white except for pale blue to show water. Apparently they were coloured by hand, paid for as piece work. It must have been a monotonous task, and a keen eye will notice the occasional lapse where 'water' has slipped beyond its usual boundaries. The maps can be found as digital scans on the National Library for Scotland's website, from which high-quality copies can be purchased.

the lower fields are mostly smaller than they are today. Back then one field near the house was divided up into five separate parcels of land delineated by a network of interconnected fences or, more likely, stone dykes. There is no trace of them now. In summer the silage machines run unimpeded from one side to the other, laying flat every blade of grass in less than 30 minutes.

The late Bryan Nelson, renowned author and seabird expert, once lived in this house and wrote his final book, *On the Rocks*, in what is now my study. He paints a vivid picture of the local mine, which operated in the mid-1800s just below the house, and what came after it:

> Who could believe that this secluded corner of rural south-west Scotland was once a rumbustious mining community? We live a little over a kilometre[11] inland of Balcary Bay guarded by whale-backed Hestan Island … In the woods below our cottage lurk deep holes from which came rock, rich with shiny black nodules of iron-ore. It was horse-carted down to Balcary Bay and shipped across the Solway to Workington on the English side. These days Tawny Owls hoot in the woods which cover the scars, now misted with Bluebells in spring. Blackcaps, Willow Warblers and, in lucky years, Pied Flycatchers and Redstarts nest here.[12]

The deep shafts are closed off now. It's difficult to believe that hundreds of tons of ore would once have been brought up from the ground and carted off across the water to England. But ironstone rocks still litter the woods, veins of pink running through them, some pieces with strange, rounded black nodules bubbling over the surface.[13] No matter how many times you pick one up, it's always heavier than you expect. Ironically perhaps, the mining industry here saved this fragment of old woodland. The uneven ground, strewn with waste rocks, and

---

[11] Wishful thinking perhaps; in fact, it is 2.5 kilometres from the house to the start of the bay.
[12] Nelson, B. (2013) *On the Rocks*. Langford Press, Peterborough.
[13] It is known as haematite or kidney ore for its reddish colour and smooth rounded surface. Some forms can apparently be ground down and used to make red paint.

the deep shafts would have been a dangerous place for livestock and impossible to cultivate. So, it was fenced off and forgotten about, and has been left mostly to its own devices for over a century. It's rewilding by accident. And it says much about the scale of human impacts on the environment that it is one of the most natural and appealing fragments of habitat that remain.

Bryan Nelson's book was published more than a decade ago. The tawny owls, the blackcaps and the willow warblers are all still here. The woods fill with the warblers' songs in spring. The owls still hoot at night, and one morning in late April this year I found their nest in a dead alder by the burn, no more than 100 metres from our house. The hole, halfway up the decaying trunk, was open on two sides, allowing light to shine through from one side to the other. Staring directly at me was one of the adults, and next to it, oblivious to the intruder in its wood, a dishevelled grey chick, unsteady on its feet.

A couple of weeks later the woods were, once again, misted with bluebells.

But not everything is the same. We haven't experienced a lucky year for redstarts or pied flycatchers, though I suspect luck has nothing to do with it. Both these birds have lost ground in recent years, and it is likely that they are gone for good.

In the 19th century, when mining was in full swing, the local wildlife would have been very different. At that time the surrounding land was largely free of planted conifers, offering a completely different prospect and missing the birds that rely on these trees. The nuthatches that now visit the garden feeders every day had yet to colonise southern Scotland, and great spotted woodpeckers, coal tits, siskins and chaffinches would all have been far less common. Kites, buzzards and other raptors should have been able to take advantage of the open country, but they didn't get the chance; by that time they were already either extinct or much depleted through persecution by farmers and gamekeepers.

The first national atlas of breeding birds was published in 1976, providing a snapshot from roughly 50 years ago. Flicking through it, I can get an idea of the changes that have taken place here within my own lifetime. On the positive side I can now watch red kites, collared doves, nuthatches and siskins, all of which were absent five decades ago. But the gains are outweighed by the losses. I may never see redstarts or pied flycatchers breeding in the woods by the house. And it's unlikely I will ever find nesting black grouse, grey partridge, corncrake, lapwing, curlew, snipe, redshank or willow tits on my walks into the surrounding countryside. Yet in the 1970s (when I was a young child growing up in England), all would have been familiar birds here.

Of all these birds, the curlew is the biggest absence for me. The odd bird still flies in from the coast in winter and early spring, settling in a field to feed for a while. But as a breeding bird it has gone, pushed out by the regular silage cutting on the lower ground and the plantations up in the hills. The bird lives on for now in at least one of our local song thrushes; it starts one of its phrases with a perfect imitation of a curlew. If I've not been paying attention, it has me looking up and around, in hope, before I realise I've been had. Again. How long will it be before even the song thrushes forget?

* * *

Occasionally I stumble across something that once belonged to Bryan Nelson in one of the outbuildings. There is an old wooden trunk, marked simply 'Nelson, To England', which must have been used to ship possessions back from one of his many overseas expeditions. And there is what looks like the nameplate from a boat, SULA, carved into a varnished piece of wood. *Sula* is the boat that serves Bass Rock in the Firth of Forth, over on the east side of Scotland, a place with which Bryan had a strong association during his long-term studies of gannets.[14] Perhaps the nameplate is from one of the forerunners of the current vessel.

From the south side of the house, we can look out across Balcary (or Auchencairn) Bay, the embarkation point for the iron ore on its journey to England. I sometimes set up the telescope in the bedroom and scan the two final layers in this landscape: the mudflats of the bay,

---

14 *Sula bassana* was once the scientific name for the northern gannet. These days it is *Morus bassanus*. Bryan Nelson published two books on the gannet, including a full-length monograph on the species: Nelson, B. (1978) *The Gannet*. Poyser, Berkhamsted.

and the wide expanse of the Solway beyond. It's too far away for any serious sea-watching, though there is one bird that because of its size and striking black-and-white plumage would be readily identifiable through the 'scope.[15] I can't help wondering if Bryan Nelson ever looked out for gannets during his time here, and if so, whether he ever managed to see one.

I've yet to see a gannet from the house, though I'll keep looking. It's left to the gulls to connect us to the bay. They roost on the sea at night (or at their nests during the breeding season) and spend much of the day patrolling the coastal waters. But each morning, groups of them, mostly herring and lesser black-backed gulls, but common and black-headed gulls too, drift up the glen in noisy, spiralling circles in search of good fields in which to feed. They are looking especially for grass where slurry has recently been spread, in expectation of a bonanza of dead and dying earthworms. Some days they seem to know where they're going, and ragged arrows of birds point purposefully inland, presumably aiming for a field they've recently visited and know will be productive. If I've not heard a hooting tawny owl or a pheasant coughing into the early morning, the gulls are often the first birds I become aware of each day. They bring the sound of the sea, pulling it closer and stitching together two of the most disparate layers of this landscape: the dull, muddy waters of the Solway and the bright, manicured green of the grass fields.

---

15 As I was writing this chapter I came across a Twitter exchange suggesting (reliably, I believe) that gannets can be identified from over 10 miles away in good conditions.

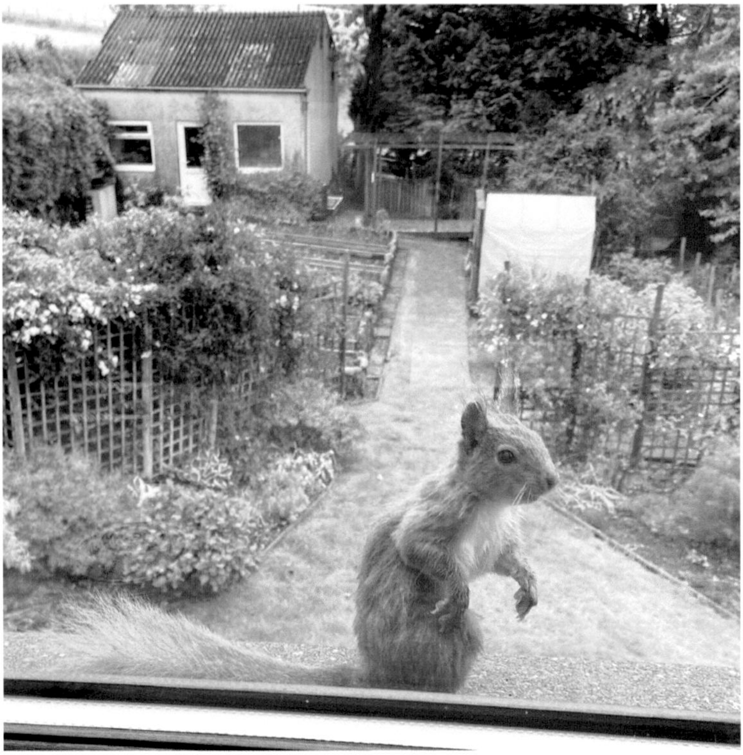

4

Squirrel wars - life on the front line

An animal that, for now, lights up the garden, and another we live in fear of seeing.

As an ornithologist, devoting a whole chapter to a mammal doesn't come easily to me. But if any animal deserves the attention, it's this one. It's an endearing creature, effortlessly winning the affection of anyone who spends time with it. Until the 20th century it would have been familiar to us all, as it shared our landscapes across the length and breadth of Britain. But it is having a tough time and is already long gone from most of its range. Near-universal popularity offers no guarantee that the remaining fragmented populations will survive, though what a tragedy it would be to lose them. Galloway is at the forefront of the bloody battle to save this animal. And we have inadvertently found ourselves on the front line.

The main problem faced by the red squirrel is an unusual one: the introduced North American grey squirrel has pushed it out from most of Britain, and threatens to do the same in its last refuges, mostly in the northern half of the country. The grey is a larger, more robust, animal. It lives at higher densities than the red, and competes with it for food. Worse still, it carries a disease, squirrel pox, to which it is resistant but which is deadly for the native animal. Wherever the two animals meet, the disease can be passed on.

In our new home we were quickly brought under the red squirrel's spell, and it even played a role in helping us choose to live here. As mentioned earlier, when we first viewed the house one appeared on the patio, holding us transfixed. When we moved in a few months later we had the usual worries about whether the boiler would work and the integrity of the roof. But, above everything else, we wanted to know one thing: do the red squirrels still visit the garden?

We needn't have worried. We learnt that the previous owners had fed them over many years, and from our first day here it was clear that this was just as much the squirrels' garden as it was ours. At any one time there are as many as five or six different animals visiting regularly, some of which we come to recognise as individuals from the variable colours (of the tails especially) or even quirks of behaviour.

The squirrels skitter about the place with near-contempt for its human inhabitants. They can appear almost anywhere around the house and garden, and even inside the garage, where they clamber about among the watering cans and flower pots. They regularly help themselves to things we were rather hoping to save for our own pleasure. In mid-summer, the strawberry patch is raided with impunity. I watch on as another intruder skips merrily away across the garden with one of the larger ripe berries before carrying it up to the garage roof or into the trees to eat, as if butter wouldn't melt …

The house has an outer coating of roughcast. For the squirrels, it's as good as bark. Leave a few peanuts on any of the window ledges, even upstairs, and they will be found and consumed. The squirrels have learnt that the rectangular blue tin we keep by the sliding patio doors means food. They know what it looks (and sounds) like, and even come running towards it if they are sufficiently hungry. After years of feeding, they have developed a strong sense of entitlement. When the food runs out, they stare in through the window with a look that combines sadness with irresistible appeal; if you have a dog, you'll know it well.

The squirrels' social interactions are interesting to watch, though frustratingly difficult to untangle. At times, two or three will sit quietly together on the small patio, all contentedly nibbling on a nut. On another day the appearance of a second animal sparks unbridled fury in the incumbent. There is angry chittering, and a frenetic chase ensues, sometimes ending up in the canopy of the sycamore trees at the back of the garden. Are these animals rivals, one trying to drive the other away? Or, as with the brown hares in the local fields, are the intentions sometimes more amorous: a male trying to show just how fast and manoeuvrable he is, chasing a female who's only too happy to put him to the test? The line between flirtation and aggression is sometimes a fine one. For young animals, these chases are best seen as play, perhaps often between siblings reared in the same drey, helping them to build the speed and manoeuvrability that will be needed in later life.

Whatever the motives, they can be difficult to watch, both from a practical perspective and as a test of nerve. They are so fast that the human eye struggles to keep pace; you end up staring hopelessly at a patch of foliage from which they have already departed. And when they are high above the ground, you genuinely fear for their safety as one animal flings itself after the other; one tiny slip would surely be fatal.

Occasionally, early in the season, before an uneasy truce develops, the returning swallows keep the squirrels on their toes, diving at them when they cross the lawn or rest for a moment out in the open. The swallows nest in the outbuildings and are alert to the potential threat from predators. In response, a squirrel will deploy its ever-useful tail, wrapping it tightly over the body, with the end poking up vertically above its head. On cold days the tail helps to retain heat, providing a windbreak and a thick layer of insulation. Now it serves an entirely different purpose; should an especially bold swallow make contact it will strike nothing but fluff.

The red squirrels are a delight. But only a few days after we moved in, we knew we had a problem. Two grey squirrels were also visiting the garden. Knowing the backstory, we felt we had no choice but to harden our hearts and do something about it. We took advice from the local Solway Forests Red Squirrel Group, and deployed a cage trap baited with food. When an animal goes inside, it depresses a plate that springs shut the entrance door. We should have guessed what would happen: the inquisitive and resourceful reds wandered into the trap readily. They could be released immediately and doing so revealed an interesting side to their character we'd not seen before. When confined to the trap with what they no doubt perceived as a predator walking towards them, they showed real aggression, throwing themselves at the wire, teeth exposed, a menacing hissed growl forced out between them.

A reminder, should we have needed one, that these are wild animals.

The greys, as required by Sod's law, were more reticent, clambering about on top of the trap, sniffing at the food below, but stubbornly refusing to enter. In the end my old air rifle was wheeled out to do the job. I killed them both in turn from an upstairs window, as they sat at the peanut feeder – forcing myself to look at the magnified image in the gun-sight when lining up the shot, and then trying not to look once it had been taken. A few weeks later a third intruder was dealt with in the same way. We hear reports that greys are now seen in gardens in the village of Auchencairn, a couple of miles away. If they start to breed in the local woods, it will become very difficult to stop them from spreading and increasing further.

Knowing there were greys about we lived in fear of seeing signs of disease in the red squirrels. At first there were no problems. They all appeared healthy and we started to relax.

Then, one late spring afternoon, I was doing battle with a battalion of ground elder marching out from the hedge into one of the flowerbeds. It's a thankless, never-ending task, but with a blackcap singing from the woods and a cuckoo piping up intermittently on the far side of the glen it was hardly taxing. Another stem snapped off at the root, leaving the bulk of the plant lying there in the soil, ready to renew its assault. I turned away, and noticed one of the squirrels on the patio. It didn't look right. Even at a distance it was somehow not as bright-eyed and perky as usual. When I walked over, all became clear. It had swollen, half-closed eyes, sores on its feet and a sorry-looking, threadbare tail. It finally moved as I walked up to it, but it was pathetically hesitant and sluggish as it scrambled desperately up the wall of the house. I sought advice from local experts, before deciding to trap it and put it out of its misery.[16]

All is not lost in the fight for red squirrels. Control efforts continue in key parts of the country to reduce the number of grey squirrels and prevent them from spreading to new areas. Novel techniques

---

16 The chances of recovery are very slim, and a diseased animal faces a protracted demise before it finally succumbs. During that time, it can transmit the virus to healthy animals.
I took the body to a local vet who sent it away so it could be tested for the virus. At the time of writing I have yet to hear the results.

might help in future. An oral contraceptive is one option, currently the subject of encouraging research and trials. Another possibility is a vaccine for the red squirrel, and there are hopeful signs that some reds may already have natural immunity to squirrel pox.

As pine martens continue to recover from past persecution, they may tip the balance in favour of the red squirrel. Reds have lived with them for centuries, and are well adapted for coexistence, recognising when they are nearby – probably through scent – so they can be extra vigilant. The North American greys don't share this history. They are more naïve and fearless, and so more likely to become prey. They may also be less able to avoid capture when chased. Grey squirrels are larger and heavier than reds, which makes it more difficult for them to retreat to the thin outer branches of the canopy where the martens would struggle to follow. In parts of Scotland, boxes are now being installed to help encourage the spread of the pine marten.

After our incident brought the reality of this struggle so close to home and especially when we heard about other cases in nearby villages, we feared the worst. But thankfully, so far, outbreaks of disease have remained sporadic, and most of the animals that live around us have remained healthy.

* * *

There is another disease that will have repercussions for the squirrels. The woodland along the burn is dominated by old ash trees. If, as seems inevitable, they succumb to ash die-back, then the woods will disappear or at least be altered dramatically, with the loss of the largest and most impressive trees. The ash unfurls its leaves later in the spring than other deciduous trees. Each year I wait patiently and celebrate their appearance, knowing that the trees will be with us for one more summer at least. In the longer term, the only hope is that some of the trees will have natural resistance to the disease.

We learn to live with change that has already happened. And it's not too difficult. Not really. I wish that corncrakes and curlews still bred locally so that I could listen out for their return each spring. I wish that their evocative, if very different, songs could still be heard in this glen.

I wish that the old woods still had their redstarts and pied flycatchers. But I don't feel these losses keenly or mourn the passing of these birds; I haven't had the opportunity. Dealing with shifting baselines is easy enough once the lines have already moved on; we do it all the time. But watching on as the line shifts before your eyes is something else. To live here while the red squirrel slowly dwindles to extinction and the old ash woods begin to fall apart would not be easy. If the worst does happen, the next owners of this house won't miss the trees or the squirrels. But the baselines will have moved on again. The ratchet of dwindling biodiversity will have tightened another couple of notches.

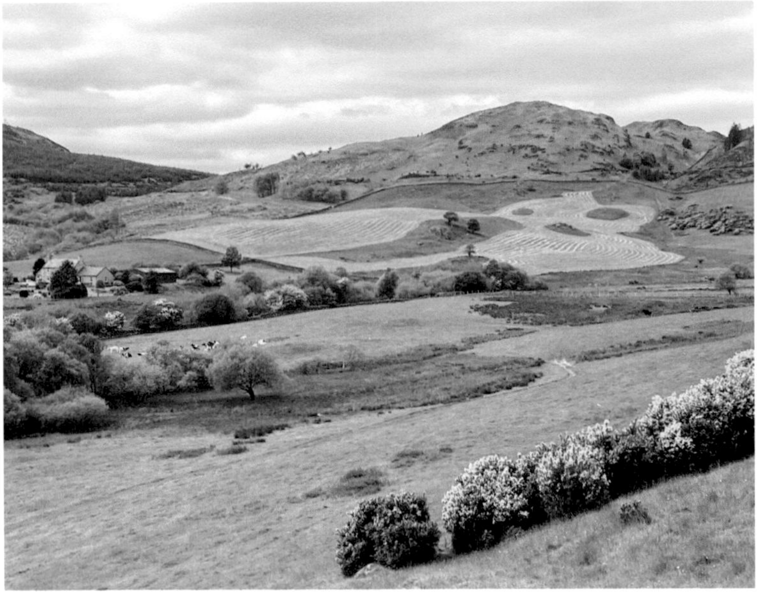

5

Wildness on the farm

Seeking out the wilder places in a heavily modified landscape.

One of the reasons Hazel and I moved to Galloway was the wild feel to the place. There is space here. Drive almost anywhere, look in almost any direction, and there are hills fading into the distance, inviting exploration. Galloway has huge tracts of land where you can walk all day and not see another soul. My time in Devon was spent searching for the surviving wild fragments in a sea of countryside dominated by humanity and its infrastructure; such places were still to be found, with a little effort. But Galloway's wild landscapes are on a different scale. There may be no wilderness left, but there is 'wildness' here in abundance.

Not everywhere in Galloway is rich in wildlife, of course. For all its space and its low population density, the landscapes here, as everywhere else in Britain, have been altered by humans – subverted to our will to a greater or lesser extent. On the lower ground, modern agriculture has swept away the natural vegetation and replaced it with meadows and pastures. In the most intensive fields the grass is so lush and dominant that at a distance it almost glows green. In the uplands, farming of a different kind takes up much of the space. Some of the slopes are still grazed by livestock, but the main crop now is timber; over the last century, vast ranks of North American trees have marched across the hills, changing their character dramatically.

Mine House is not far from the boundary between the improved farmland on the lower ground and the patchily afforested slopes above. Walk in either direction up the sides of the glen, and within ten minutes you'll reach an ancient stone dyke. On the near side is pasture, close-cropped by sheep and cattle. Here, the walking is easy. Hop across to the other side, and in summer you risk disappearing into an impenetrable tangle of bracken, heather and brambles at the edge of the hill country.

* * *

When walking through landscapes I sometimes find myself thinking in terms of a 'scale of wildness', even trying to come up with a score to reflect the extent of human intervention: the more humans have messed with a place, the lower the number. An urban park might get a point if it has a few trees. Farmland can score a few points if there is space for wild flowers, pockets of native woodland and decent hedges. To experience a ten, a visit to one of the national parks in a country that takes the term seriously would be needed – the United States or Canada, for example. There, you can walk for hours through natural vegetation, and when doing so you'll need to keep a wary eye out for the top predators that still call it home. But I've not had that pleasure for many years. The very best that Britain has to offer might creep up to a six, or even a seven if I'm feeling generous.

But let's start near the bottom, close to the house, where the grass fields are intensively managed. Only since living here have I fully appreciated the extent of human intervention required to maintain these fields. From late winter through to the end of summer, something is done to them every few days. In early spring the fields are chain-harrowed; a grid of metal tines (like a giant rake) is dragged along to break up the turf, helping to remove dead grass and improve drainage. Then comes the heavy roller, passing back and forth, flattening out molehills, pushing down stones that might otherwise damage cutting blades, and (so I'm told, though I still find it difficult to believe) encouraging the grass to tiller and so produce multiple new shoots. When it's done, each field wears immaculate stripes; they are like vast lawns, a good deal neater than the small patch of grass on our side of the hedge.

On another day, clouds of pinkish-white lime billow out behind a spreader, before settling to the ground where the dust will reduce the acidity of the soil. If the field gets too weedy it will be topped to cut off the unwanted plants and prevent them from setting seed, or sprayed with a herbicide to kill them. A bright red tanker appears regularly, hauled into the fields to dribble lines of dark, enriching slurry across the sward. Every so often a field that has become too weedy will be sprayed with herbicide, raked smooth and then reseeded with grass.

At least twice each summer the grass in some of the fields is cut and collected into long lines with an unfathomable contraption pulled behind the tractor. It's made up of a series of whisks which contrive to spin the grass on either side inwards into a neat line in the centre. Then it can be scooped up and funnelled into a trailer skilfully keeping pace alongside. Fully loaded, the trailers rattle off down the track to the silage store, returning empty by a different route across the fields – wagons circling to ensure that they don't get in each other's way and the frenetic pace of the harvest is maintained. The next day, all is quiet. Cows might be moved onto the cut fields for a few days. They hoover up cut grass that has been spilt, and wander along the edges, eating vegetation that the great machines have been unable to reach.

There have been other surprises too: the fields are grazed at times by a bewildering combination of different animals. Pull up the blinds in the morning and you never know quite what will be there in the nearest field. One day sheep and cattle are mixed in together. The next, the sheep have gone and it's just cattle. Three days later it's still cattle, but instead of full-grown dairy cows it's a pack of boisterous young bullocks or heifers, merrily galloping around along the fence-line to establish the limits of their new, temporary home. A week later the cows are back – but this time there's a huge, thick-set bull pacing methodically from one to the next, and our regular dog walk is duly re-routed. Every few days, something different.

Twice a day, the cows walk down to the milking parlour, the reluctant ones nudged along with shouts of encouragement from a quad bike rider sweeping up at the rear. The track to the village runs through the farmyard. But sometimes when the cows are in the parlour, two gates are closed so they can cross the track and get back to the fields without wandering off, either towards the village or the other way up towards our house. Soon after we moved here, Hazel tried to get the car through, but a group of cows emerged before she could close the first gate. Unresponsive to shooing noises and a panicked whirling of arms, off they marched up the track. There was no one around, and as Hazel was running late she had no choice but to leave them to it. When she saw Louis later, he was very understanding.

Now, though, we know the drill. The cows are milked in groups of ten; once finished, each group ambles out of the door, crosses the track and heads out into the field, sometimes with a playful jump or two if it's early summer and fresh grass is still a novelty. Once the tenth animal is safely across you have a minute or two to get the car through before the next group begins to emerge. It's tight, but it's doable: open the first gate, drive through, close it again, run to the second gate (dodging the fresh cowpats), open it, run back to the car (avoiding the dung again), drive through, close the gate behind you. Job done.

The animals are sometimes limited to part of a field, to focus their grazing. This, I've learnt, is 'mob grazing'. Each day, a temporary electric fence is moved to open up a different section of the field. It's designed to simulate how grasslands would once have been grazed naturally, with herds of animals bunched closely together to guard against predators, before moving on to a new area as the vegetation is depleted. Each pulse of activity breaks up the sward, fertilises the grass and then gives it a chance to regrow for a while with no animals present to check its progress. This allows plants to develop resilient roots, and grass production is apparently improved compared to more traditional grazing. Occasionally, just before the cattle arrive, the grass is cut, leaving it piled into lines across the field. This is another attempt to maximise production. The cows eat all the grass in the clippings, rather than feeding selectively by seeking out only the best-quality leaves. And once all the old growth has been cleared away by the animals the grass can regrow strongly. My old mental image of cows being let out into the fields in spring and left pretty much to themselves (milking aside) for the summer has had to go.

How much of this activity is guided by a meticulous plan, drawn up for the summer ahead, I wonder? And how much is day-to-day juggling based on the condition of the animals and an assessment of how the grass is looking?

These fields nearest our house are close to being monocultures of grass. A few docks and thistles might find their way in for a while, and there are patches of flowering clover to break up the monotony, but very few wild flowers can survive here. New plants trying to grow are soon swamped by fast-growing, slurry-fuelled grass, well adapted to regrow rapidly from the base. Plants that try to compete are soon grazed or cut into oblivion. Usually, there is not much wildlife here. I see the occasional brown hare, fox or roe deer passing through, but often that's all they are doing; they are on their way to another place where there is more cover, more variety and more chance of finding a meal. A brown hare might loiter for a while and nibble on something that catches its eye, but it will need to look elsewhere for a safe place to rear its young.

There are times, though, when even these fields burst into life. Whenever a mob of cattle is grazing close to the house, the swallows nesting in our outbuildings take full advantage, sometimes joined by a few house martins and a sand martin or two from the colony nearby. They weave elegant, sweeping lines through the herd, keeping close to the ground and hoovering up flies attracted by the animals and their skitters of dung. The large, brown dung-flies are the most obvious arrivals. They swarm about the fresh pats, materialising almost before the liquid has slopped down onto the ground, and flying up into dangerous airspace as the cows move about in the field. Small dung-beetles follow not far behind, peppering the pats with holes as they begin to solidify.

When the grass is cut there is another bonanza. Corvids, gulls and raptors appear as if by magic. They might see what's happening as they fly overhead, but they also keep an eye on each other, noticing when their compatriots drop down to feed. That way, birds can home in on good feeding places from afar. Recent studies have hinted at the possibility that smell might also play a role. Researchers in Europe found that white storks quickly appeared at cut fields from downwind, even though visual cues were not available to them.[17] A fake cut-grass smell sprayed onto fields also attracted storks. Is it possible that gulls, corvids and birds of prey might also use the same cues?

---

17 Wikelski, M. et al. (2021) 'Smell of green leaf volatiles attracts white storks to freshly cut meadows.' *Scientific Reports* 11: Article number 12912.

On a field cut in late April, I watched hundreds of birds, including herring and lesser black-backed gulls, carrion crows, jackdaws, two red kites and a lone buzzard. April is early for silage cutting (there was ice on my windscreen that morning) and the large numbers of birds probably reflected the lack of alternative options. Early another morning I watched as a fox walked slowly between lines of grass cut the previous evening, pausing regularly to investigate potential food items.

It is difficult to be sure exactly what is being consumed in recently cut silage fields. I suspect it is small mammals or even invertebrates killed and injured by the cutting process, and easy to spot once the grass has been trimmed. And when the cut is very short and the ground is damp, bare soil can be exposed, which makes earthworms accessible. These feeding frenzies don't last long, but no matter; there is always another field. In dry summer weather, the lowlands of Galloway hum to the sound of grass cutters, twirlers and gatherers, and for animals that have learnt to take advantage there is a good living to be made.

Slurry-spreading offers another bonanza for the same group of animals. The modern apparatus involves up to 50 flexible pipes connected to a tanker, each of which drizzles a line of slurry onto the grass as the tractor moves forward. A large field can be covered in dark stripes, a few inches apart, in not much more than an hour. Once again, birds see (or smell?) the opportunity and sweep in from far and wide. This time the attraction is earthworms. These improved fields are rich in worms, but the slurry kills or incapacitates those near the surface. Thousands are affected by each application, and gulls, especially, sometimes four different species, are adept at strolling across the field, picking them off one by one. I've watched herring gulls and lesser black-backs averaging around five successful pecks a minute, each worm quickly manipulated in the bill before being gobbled down. Fieldfares flock to these fields in late winter, presumably attracted by the same thing, along with a few blackbirds, song thrushes and, close to the hedges, even the occasional robin. Foxes also take advantage, and I suspect that badgers do too, under cover of darkness; earthworms form an important part of the diet of both animals.

These frenetic bouts of activity are fun to watch, and they show that even intensively managed fields support wildlife. But this is not necessarily all good news. Many of the creatures benefitting here are adaptable generalists that do well in a countryside heavily modified by humans. And they are predators as well as scavengers. The worry is that their numbers might be boosted to artificially high levels by all this extra food, in fields that provide little useful habitat for other wildlife. The problems for beleaguered ground-nesting songbirds and waders are compounded: they can't nest in fields that are cut so often, and when they seek out other places to breed they have to contend with an inflated population of nest predators. For our most vulnerable birds, it has all been too much. If I want to find breeding lapwings, curlews or snipe then driving to a nature reserve is now the best option. They no longer nest in the fields close to home.

* * *

Not all the pastures are managed this way. The shape and underlying geology of the terrain has spared some of the land from the most intensive interventions.

Where there are rocky outcrops or steep slopes, we get a glimpse back in time to how things once were. Ironically perhaps, the scale of modern farming equipment has helped. Where the land is flat and free of obstacles the huge machines are brutally efficient, but they are not designed to clamber about on steep slopes, or pick their way delicately between outcrops of rock or scattered trees and bushes. So in these places no slurry or fertiliser is added to help the grass grow. And no spinning blades arrive to skim the heads from the plants before they can flower. There are livestock in summer, but grazing levels are lower here, as the animals tend to keep to the places where the living is easier.

What a difference this makes! The vegetation stands out clearly from the rest of the fields. It is a more natural yellowy-green colour, lacking the bright, artificial glow of the improved grass. But if it looks less vivid and intense from a distance, everything changes when you begin to walk through it. Now, the variety of colours is striking. In spring there is a haze of bluebells, and a couple of months later drifts of pale blue harebells emerge.[18] There are the yellows of lady's bedstraw, catsear, buttercup and tormentil, and the frothy white flowerheads of meadowsweet, pignut and yarrow. Even the rocks here grow flowers. Carpets of English stonecrop creep out across them, clusters of perfect pink stars held up above the sprawling mats of leaves. And in small fissures, the bold purple of bell heather on bonsai bushes that seem to sprout directly from the granite.

The edge of one field has a small burn running through it and has been spared from intensive management by its steep banks, and in the flatter areas by the waterlogged, boggy ground. Both help to keep the machines away. Here, the vegetation is studded with the spikes of bog asphodels, yellow at first, changing to a fiery orange later in the summer, and hundreds of heath spotted orchids, scattering pale pink into the colour scheme.

In these places I find myself interacting with the land rather than simply tramping across it. There is sufficient diversity of life that lots of little detours are required to investigate interesting plants or one of the many invertebrates that make use of them. Flat stones are worth turning over carefully to reveal the red or black ant nests beneath them and, if your luck is in, a slow worm threading itself through the ant tunnels as it retreats from the intrusion. I pick and chew the fresh, acidic leaves of common sorrel. Low-growing thyme plays with my compulsion to pull a few leaves and rub them between my fingers to release the scent. In late summer I'll be back to gather field mushrooms, snacking on the small white buttons as I walk, and to marvel at the bright yellow, orange and crimson waxcap fungi scattered liberally about the turf.

There is another fungus that grows here in late summer, until the first frosts of autumn. I've learnt to look out for it having read Michael Pollan's eye-opening book *How to Change Your Mind*. He describes (and then demonstrates) how the chemicals in liberty caps dissolve the human ego and provide lasting therapeutic benefits.[19] Research

---

18 The naming of certain plants can become tricky when you move from England to Scotland (or vice versa). While harebells are usually called bluebells north of the border, so the bluebell – the plant that carpets the local woods in May – is known as the wild hyacinth. I've stuck with what I know best, with apologies for any confusion.
19 Pollan, M. (2018) *How to Change Your Mind: The New Science of Psychedelics*. Penguin Books.

into psilocybin began in the 1950s, but was stymied by apprehensive governments when psychedelics leaked out from the laboratories into popular culture. Recently it has started up again, in what you'd hope are more enlightened (and perhaps more urgent) times, and psilocybin shows great promise as a treatment for depression and other long-term illnesses. If I can only muster the courage, I might indulge in a little research of my own.

But pockets of vegetation like this are not enough for the vulnerable ground-nesting birds I mentioned earlier. The problem is one of scale. These birds need substantial areas of good habitat to successfully hide their eggs and young from predators. So I must make do instead with birds that drop in for a while to feed. The green woodpecker is the most striking visitor, though as it is the colour of grass it is easy to overlook. When it flies up, it gives itself away, and just in case you miss it, its raucous, laughing calls guide the eyes in the right direction. Like all woodpeckers, it flies in a series of bounds, propelled skywards with a burst of flapping, then arcing back towards the ground before another flurry of wing-beats fires it upwards again and back on course. Its young are secure within the woods, inside a hole chiselled into an old ash tree. But they will be raised on invertebrates from the meadows. Ants are a favourite food, and the bare earth of exposed ant hills shows where they have been raided, the hapless occupants pulled out with a long, sticky tongue, perfectly designed for the job.

Earlier today I rested for a while on a rocky hummock in the middle of a field. An island of variety and colour in a sea of monotonous green. I sat among a drift of harebells, each flower nodding in the breeze as if in earnest conversation with its neighbours. They have plenty to talk about: the name hints at an association between plant and animal and, true to form, I often see hares in these meadows. An alternative name of witch bell is also suggestive of links between the two species: witches, having sampled the juice of the plant, were said to transform into hares.

Butterflies added their own splashes of colour to the scene. A small copper landed on the ground, flashing bright orange as its wings flicked open, and a dapper male common blue hurried by. Peacocks and small tortoiseshells floated languidly from one thistle flower to the next, and with them a worn, tatty-looking dark green fritillary. A small heath flapped weakly above the turf giving the impression that staying airborne was a constant struggle.

Experiencing all this and then looking out across the rest of the farm I had what felt in the moment like a minor epiphany, although now, transferred to the page, it is nothing but a tired statement of the blindingly obvious. A few decades ago, when our countryside was manged less intensively, the whole glen (and many others like it) would have looked like the small patch of ground where I'd been resting. What a sight it must have been!

These days, if you are an ornithologist who aspires to learn the names of a few more wild flowers, if you enjoy walking through meadows where grasshoppers leap up from your feet with every step, if you want to watch myriad butterflies and bees skip from one plant to the next, or if you habitually snack on edible leaves or mushrooms as you walk, then it is to one of these small surviving scraps of land that you must come.

I climbed down from my vantage point and walked back towards the house, shoving my boots through the thick grass. Away from my rocky island, the only colour now was green. There were no sounds from invertebrates, no interesting smells – nothing worth pausing for, to look at more closely. What, I wondered, does the future hold for the last fragments of flower-rich meadow? What if they too are swept away in the name of ever greater efficiency? It has already happened across much of Galloway's lowlands. The rocks have been ripped out, and the slopes and hillocks levelled to make way for uniform sheets of grass and the huge machines that tend to them.

We've seen this scenario play out in a field of rough, tree-studded pasture on the way to Dalbeattie, our nearest town. Over several months, dozens of mature trees have been felled, cut up and removed, and the boulders that once littered the slope have been grubbed out and gathered into piles. It wasn't an exceptional place for wildlife, which explains why it had no legal protection. But there was space enough here for a wide range of animals and plants. It was a place that looked worthy of exploration, and I'd often thought of pulling the car over and having a closer look. But all that's left now is a smooth surface of dark, rock-free soil, no doubt soon to be seeded with grass. There has been much discussion recently about 'rewilding' and how we might begin to restore some of the rough, wild places that have been lost. And yet the destruction of wildlife-rich habitats that have somehow survived against all odds continues. If we can't spare what little is left of our wildlife-rich habitats, then *restoration* feels like a distant and unlikely goal.

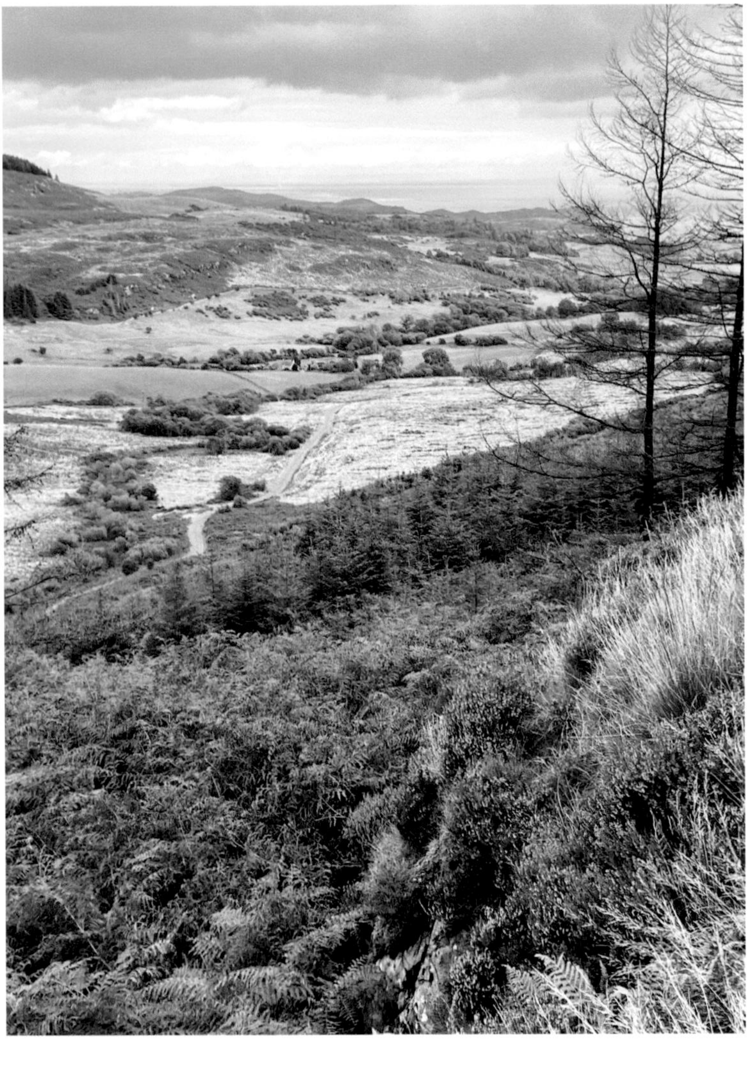

6

Wildness in the hills

Escaping humanity beneath the Sitka spruce trees and the wilder land of the open hills.

When the mood strikes and I have a few hours to spare, I walk further from the house, off the farmland and away into the surrounding hills. The farm boundary is the old stone dyke that runs along the top of the pasture fields. To climb a little higher up the wildness scale all I need do is clamber over to the other side.

While there is more wildness above the dyke, this is a mixed and complex landscape; a mish-mash of the wild and the artificial, the self-willed and the planted. The gentler slopes are mostly covered in conifers originating from the west coast of North America. They have been installed, one after the other, by human hands. Now, there are millions of them, in long rows, each one just a couple of metres away from its nearest neighbours. A few different kinds of tree can be found here, but one is dominant: the Sitka spruce. Named after a place in Alaska, it thrives in Galloway's wet climate and poor upland soils. It looks like a Christmas tree, but unlike the Norway spruce (the familiar tree we bring into our homes) the Sitka's whorls of needles are sharp and spiky rather than soft and family-friendly, with a distinctive bluish tinge to the undersides. If in doubt, try grasping one of the outer branches firmly in your hand; if you can do it without flinching then it's not a Sitka spruce.

These plantations are odd places. I find myself drawn back to them every so often, even though they don't support much wildlife. Partly it's the near-total absence of other people. If part of the meaning of 'wildness' is that humans don't have a strong influence on the land on a *day-to-day* basis then these forests fit the bill. Here are square miles of land where, most days, there is no one else present. True, when a new area is planted (or replanted after felling) there are bursts of activity. But after each one, the next pulse of management won't be for another 30 or 40 years, when the time comes to harvest the trees. In the decades between planting and felling, the forest is left to itself.

If you've never done it before, it's worth experiencing the interior of a well-grown Sitka spruce plantation. You'll need to push your way through the narrow rows of trees, trying to avoid sharp jabs from the foliage. On a stifling July day it will be refreshingly cool among the trees. And in January, when a gale is biting through four layers of clothing out in the open, there will be barely a disturbance of the air at ground level within the plantation.

The trees are so close together that little light finds its way to the ground. That, and the thick layer of dead needles, makes it difficult for anything else to grow. It's more crop than forest, and not many birds are able to eke out a living. You might hear coal tits and goldcrests, and perhaps the odd chaffinch and siskin. Often, though, it will be eerily silent. Calm and tranquillity can be found beneath the trees, lending these places an unexpectedly serene and powerful atmosphere. With the gloomy light, the stillness of the air and sightlines closed off on all sides, it can feel as if the rest of the world has ceased to exist. Even the few planes passing high overhead don't seem as intrusive as usual. They serve only to emphasise that *out there*, beyond the foliage, is another world entirely – far away and, for now at least, irrelevant. Perhaps, as an enthusiast for wildlife, you'll find it depressing. Perhaps your thoughts will be drawn to all the wildlife that would have been present on the moors before being swept away by the trees. You might even be spooked by the experience, so different is it from the everyday. But if you are seeking a little escapism, it's not a bad way to spend a few minutes.

To return to more open sightlines, following one of the old stone dykes is a good option. As well as separating the hill country from the farms below, they also wind for endless miles between the blocks of conifers, a poignant reminder that these slopes were once farmed for livestock rather than for timber. They are obsolete now, but they have held up remarkably well over the decades. Where there are gaps,

I suspect that foresters are responsible; the dykes have probably been dismantled to allow an easy passage from one side to the other during tree-planting. These lines of stones provide narrow bands through the dense forests where light reaches the ground, and heather, bracken and other plants have taken full advantage. Underneath the trees, footsteps fall upon a thin, lifeless carpet of dead spruce needles. But alongside the dykes, you must battle through luxuriant vegetation.

For an easier stroll, there are always the forest tracks. Built for the timber lorries and harvesters that appear every few decades when there is planting or felling to be done, they see almost no traffic during the long intervals in between. As with the stone dykes, there is more wildlife here, because there is more light. On the wide verges, native plants and shrubs thrive, adding variety to the monoculture of conifers. In spring, willow warblers and whitethroats sing from the bushes, and small pearl-bordered fritillaries cruise by on stiff wings, searching for flowers rich in nectar or violets on which to lay their eggs. In spring and autumn, these tracks are good places for migrant birds. Spotted flycatchers loop through the air after insects, using the bushes as lookout posts, and a redstart might shimmer its tail from an exposed perch before slipping back into cover. Where brambles have grown up, the fruits attract thrushes and blackcaps, and willow warblers make short work of the flies drawn in by the ripe berries.

The tracks themselves provide habitat. There are so few vehicles that foxgloves, willowherbs and other plants spring up from the barren surface. And where there is little vegetation, creatures that require bare substrates can make a good living. Green tiger beetles scurry over the ground, seeking out prey to run down and grasp with their outsized jaws. Often, they fly up ahead of me before I've seen them, pitching back down a little further along the track. And there are two butterflies here that love bare ground and the opportunities it presents to warm up quickly when the sun comes out. The dingy skipper appears in May and June, seeking yellow-flowering bird's-foot trefoil, its main food plant. As the name implies, this small butterfly is drab and inconspicuous, and easy to dismiss as a day-flying moth, if you notice it at all. Nationally it is in decline, but these forest tracks provide a refuge.

Later in the summer, on warm days, the larger, more common, grayling is a frequent companion. I associate it mainly with coastal sites, but here, a few miles inland, the forest roads offer similar bare ground to the rocks and worn footpath of the local sea-cliffs. It too is a rather drab butterfly, but it has a character and charm that is all its own. On some days it seems to exist only in the air, appearing as if by magic ahead of me, then vanishing again as it lands further along the track, even as my eyes attempt to track it; the cryptic, grey-patterned wings allow it to dissolve into its background. If you do manage to find one at rest (and it can be done) you'll notice its wings remain firmly closed, with the brighter, orange-washed forewings folded away, out of sight. To regulate its temperature, rather than basking with its wings open, it tilts its body, in a series of little jerks, so that it is at just the right angle to the sun.

For a brighter, if more commonplace, selection of butterflies, I visit a lone mature buddleia that has grown up along the edge of a track. A stray seed must have been carried into the hills years ago on a forester's boot – or perhaps more likely, given the seeds' winged design, blown up here on the wind. The abundant flowers are full of nectar and the resulting scent billows out across the hills, undetected at any distance by mere humans, but pulling in invertebrates from far and wide. This single shrub can host several dozen peacocks at a time, together with a few red admirals, small tortoiseshells and painted ladies, and even a dark green fritillary or two. At intervals they all spill up into the air due to some unseen, unknowable disturbance, before gathering their courage and resettling one by one.

* * *

Another option for walking in the open is one of the clearings where the mature spruce trees have been felled. The long, straight stems have all been carted away, dozens at a time, on the back of a forestry lorry. The work will have been done not with a chainsaw, but with a cutting device on the end of a long, flexible arm, controlled by an operator sitting inside the machine's cab. In seconds, with a minimum of fuss (and noise), the stem is severed at the base and the side branches stripped, before the arm swings away to grab its next tree. Now the ground is strewn with the wreckage. All the side branches (or brash) are here in piles or long lines across the clearing, where the next generation of trees will soon be planted. Until the new trees grow up, brash provides the only structure for birds. Tree pipits and stonechats perch prominently on top of the piles, while dunnocks and wrens creep about within them, emerging every so often before slipping away again in their ongoing quest for invertebrates.

More machines arrive before replanting – diggers this time. They spend several weeks depositing small piles of soil in narrow rows, about 2 metres apart. The trees arrive in plastic sacks, each with 200 thin, insignificant-looking saplings packed inside. You'd think a few sacks would be sufficient to cover a large area, but hundreds are needed for each clearing. It makes sense only when you consider the planting density. If trees are planted 2 metres apart then one sack (with its 200 trees) will cover an area of just 40 by 20 metres. To plant, say, a square kilometre – not an especially large area by modern forestry standards – 1,250 sacks (containing a total of 250,000 trees) will be needed.

Then follows the only intervention that still requires a human in direct contact with the soil. The planters arrive and spend weeks at a time walking up and down the long rows, stepping around the old stumps and the brash to push a tiny tree into each pile of soil. One day, while I was there when this was being done, one of the workers kindly paused for a few moments to explain the logic behind this planting technique. The earth in each heap will have been scooped up by the digger and dropped in a pile alongside the hole, so that the fertile upper layer of topsoil is at the bottom of the pile. Thus the soil from deeper in the ground, which is less fertile, sits on top; it is less likely to become overgrown with weeds that might otherwise interfere with the young tree. Then, when the trees are planted, they are pushed down so that the roots are in contact with the richest soil towards the base of the pile.

In North America this land might be called a 'tree farm', a place where a crop is grown, albeit one with a long interval between planting and harvest. That's not to denigrate such things; we all make use of the product. But it's a term that captures the nature of these places more effectively than words such as 'woodland', 'forest', or even the one I tend to use: 'plantation'. Trees are planted for all sorts of reasons; here it is so that they can be cut down when the time comes.

After a few years, the young trees will have grown up a little, and grasses and other plants now fill the gaps between them. The holes left by the diggers are largely hidden, but they remain as a hazard for the unwary; pitfall traps for humans, carefully concealed by the vegetation. More dangerous still are the drainage channels, carved out of boggy, waterlogged land. They are cut by machine to allow water to run away, drying out the soil so that it is better suited to growing trees. They are often narrow, but can be several feet deep. Plants colonise the edges and drape themselves over the gap, masking it from view; when venturing into these places it's as well to tread carefully.

While the trees remain small the replanted areas have one final wild flourish. In high summer, the slopes develop a pinkish tinge, the result of thousands of foxglove spikes, all just a little taller, for now, than the conifers. These flowers stand for everything the trees disavow. They are subject to the whims of the wind, scattered randomly – naturally – all around the rigid lines of saplings, wherever the seeds happened to settle and find things to their liking. It's quite a sight. But it won't last; once the trees are a few feet higher, they will begin to shut out the light, and a year-round veil of dark green will return. It will be another three decades before light floods down once again, and the foxgloves get another chance to shine.

Deer can damage young trees by browsing the fresh new shoots. I see plenty of roe deer in these forests, but the numbers are kept down by stalkers with high-powered, silenced rifles. Their wooden hides are dotted about the young plantations and clear-fells, and I find they can be handy places to shelter in when the weather turns. Some hides are at ground level, while others are raised up on small wooden towers, which help to provide clear sightlines across the surrounding land. If you are brave enough to clamber up the rickety ladder, they make excellent, impromptu wildlife hides as well. They are also co-opted by the local wildlife; barn owl pellets show where birds have rested between bouts of hunting, flying in through the narrow, rectangular viewing slots – perhaps, like me, taking refuge from a sudden change in the weather.

* * *

The afforested areas have their appeal (reservations aside) but the real joy of these hills, and the main reason I keep coming back, is the land that has escaped the trees. On the steepest and rockiest ground, large areas of open moorland remain. The machines couldn't easily reach these places, and in any case there is probably too little soil to make planting worthwhile. They can be tricky to reach even on foot, but burning leg muscles and a bit of scrambling are a small price to pay to experience some of the wildest land Galloway has to offer.

It's rare these days to find places where humanity has had no recent role to play. But up here, the vegetation on these surviving patches of moor is natural; nothing has been planted. Humans have not sought to influence what grows, either directly or through the grazing pressure of domestic livestock. Ironically, perhaps, it was the coming of the plantations that helped create these oases of non-intervention; livestock and young trees do not mix well, so the animals were cleared from the hills. The old stone dykes, as well as more modern fence-lines, ensure that, the odd escapee aside, they remain on the farmland below.

Two different types of vegetation dominate these places. Neither is easy to walk through, especially in high summer. In the bracken beds, the plants grow so tall that you find yourself walking *within* or even *beneath* the vegetation rather than across it. Bracken is much maligned, as it can become dominant, taking over huge areas and excluding other plants. But here, where it grows in patches surrounded by larger areas of heather, it fits well into the landscape, and it provides shelter for more delicate plants that grow beneath it. Violets do well in spots where dappled light filters down to the ground, and the dark green fritillaries that scud past every so often seek them out to lay their eggs.

Away from the bracken beds, heather takes over. Common heather, or ling, jostles for supremacy with bell heather. At its peak, in August, the land glows a deep purple from a distance; a uniform haze of colour built from billions of tiny flowers. Close up, the colours break apart; there is the deep purple of the bell heather, the pale pink ling, and, in the wetter spots, the paler, washed-out pink of cross-leaved heath. It's a treat for the eyes – and for nectar-feeding insects of all kinds. Small tortoiseshells, peacocks and painted ladies add their own colours to the scene, while bumblebees and honey bees enrich the soundscape. The honey bees must fly in from several kilometres away, from hives (or wild nests) somewhere down in the glen below.

As with the bracken, these sweeps of heather are tricky to navigate. The land is uneven and slopes steeply. There is no path, though at least here, unlike within the tallest bracken, you can see where you are going. The heather is too thick to push though, so it's a case of stepping over the low bushes and hoping to find a secure footing between them. I sometimes borrow a badger path for a while. They are narrow, but they provide an established route between the plants where the ground has been worn flat. Even so, losing balance and toppling over is an unavoidable part of the ritual, each fall cushioned by dense, springy heather.

When I walk here my thoughts often turn to rewilding. It's a hot topic among conservationists, and the term has become contentious. It means different things to different people. Broadly, though, it's about allowing natural processes a freer hand in areas set aside for wildlife. In contrast, most nature reserves are carefully managed by humans to maintain the habitats present, and the wildlife they support. Flower-rich meadows are grazed or cut to prevent them from becoming overgrown with grasses. Scrub is cleared from grassland and reedbeds to keep them from slowly morphing into woodland. Woodland itself is coppiced on a cycle to let light down to the ground so that woodland flowers, and the invertebrates they support, can thrive.

Even the idea of setting aside a particular piece of land to do its own thing is an intervention of a kind; it's a decision taken by people involving lines marked on a map, land purchase perhaps, and an expressed intention as to how best to proceed. But the moorland here between the plantations offers something subtly but delightfully different. It has not been mapped or marked out as important. There is no management plan. As far as I can tell, human decision-making has not influenced this place in the half-century or so since the foresters arrived and realised it would not do for trees. It has fallen through a gap between human endeavours: not farmed, not planted, not nature reserve – not anything really. No one else comes here. It's as free from humanity as it is possible to find in modern Britain. It is, I suppose, rewilding by default. And, as such, it is a glorious place for a solitary human to spend time.

* * *

As mentioned earlier, whenever I'm in the hills I keep a keen eye out for adders, a creature that adds its own magic to these slopes. It carries with it a hint of menace and when scrambling up the steeper ground I'm especially careful to watch where I put my hands. As far as humans are concerned it's not a dangerous animal, not really – but it can inflict a painful bite from the moment it is born. This it uses to subdue small mammals and birds that are then tracked until they succumb before being swallowed whole, though it can also bite in self-defence. Being bitten is not something I'd relish, especially out here on steep ground, with no phone signal and a long, tricky walk home. So my senses are heightened, just a little. We have done away with our truly dangerous animals; the brown bears, aurochs (or wild cattle) and other great beasts are long gone. But even on days when I don't see it (and that's most days) this enigmatic reptile helps keep my thoughts here, in this place, in the moment. And that is no bad thing.

These slopes are well suited to another reptile, the common lizard. They live up to their name here, though it's not always easy to get a good look at one; they are lightning-quick, and disappear into cover at the first hint of disturbance. It's hard to imagine anything being able to catch up with one, but if the worst happens they have a neat trick. Hazel witnessed it first hand, coming across the bizarre spectacle of a live lizard in two pieces, one of which was writhing about on the ground. It wasn't clear what had caused this; there was no likely predator nearby. But the way this defence mechanism works was obvious enough. The tail is designed to break away when grasped by the mouth or claws of an attacker. Then it wriggles, wormlike, drawing interested eyes to the least valuable part of the animal, allowing (on a good day) the head and body to slip quietly away. It works. Hazel quickly pulled out her phone to snatch a few seconds of video; it shows the wriggling tail.

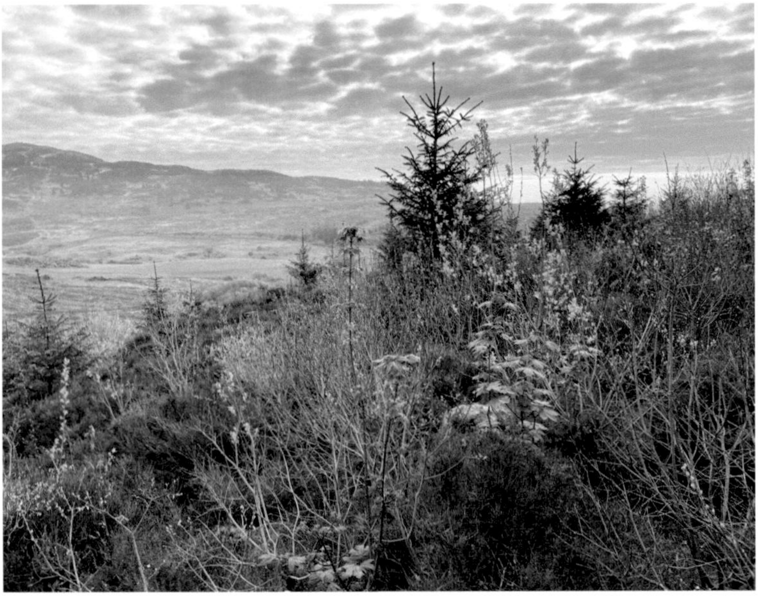

7

The new wild

A glowing beetle, an ancient fort, and trying to escape (or accept) the influence of humans.

Today's trip into the hills, with a planned overnight stay, came about because I had stumbled into a glow-worm larva here a few weeks ago, in rough grass by a newly replanted forest. Lovely to find, I thought, but does it really count as a glow-worm if I haven't seen it glow? I've not had that pleasure for over 30 years. So I've waited a few weeks hoping that my larva will have turned into an adult, along with others like it. When it's dark I'll try to find some of the females, lit up to attract a passing male. In the meantime, I have a few detours in mind to make the most of the day and the fine early June weather.

The ash woods flanking the burn offer the most attractive route up into the hills. The magic of spring is starting to ebb away. The sheets of wild garlic and bluebells have been assailed by recent rains, and many of the flowers lie flattened on the ground, the long process of decay about to begin. A few tree leaves already have pieces missing – the first scars from a battle that will rage all summer.

Not for the first time, I find myself trying to picture what it might have been like to be the first person ever to walk here. It's a game I play, the idea being to find little corners of land where there are no obvious signs that humanity exists. It's not easy. In the local countryside this old deciduous wood is the only place it can work, and even then an old sawn-off tree-stump or a glimpse of stone dyke through a gap in the foliage can easily break the spell.

The first people to make it to Britain arrived as far back as a million years ago. Once here, they (or should that be 'we'?) did their hunting and gathering while conditions were benign, but were repeatedly forced out whenever the climate cooled and ice swept back across the land. The evidence suggests this may have happened as many as eight times. After each withdrawal, as the climate ameliorated they duly recolonised Britain from their refuges in southern Europe. But there's a gap in the record. A big gap. It appears that from about 180,000 to 70,000 years ago humans failed to recolonise Britain, despite warmer conditions and a well-forested landscape. During this time, the woods were full of life, as are these woods, but people were absent.

I have science writer Caspar Henderson to thank for this potted history, and walking through these woods I share his 'deep sense of calm and happiness' when thinking about our long absence.[20] I try to imagine birds singing out to proclaim their territories year after year, for more than a hundred thousand springs, with no people to enjoy (or rudely interrupt) their music. If I were given a chance at time travel and had to pick just one period, I'd ignore the irony and I'd go back to Britain during this protracted spell of human absence. I'd roam through a pristine landscape, a landscape that no longer exists anywhere. Much of the wildlife would be familiar, but there would be no trace of human influence; no fences, dykes, cut stumps or litter, and no chance at all of bumping into another person.

Now, a willow warbler sings from low scrub at the edge of the wood; a slurred, descending chain of silver that is still a familiar sound here, despite worrying declines further south. During the millennia-long absence of humans from Britain, this species, along with other migrants, would probably have encountered humans when they headed south for the winter. In contrast, the resident birds would have remained oblivious to our existence; for over 100,000 generations the wrens, robins, blue tits and nuthatches I can hear now would have had no concept of what a human was.

There were compensations, of course. While missing out on humans, those birds might have been familiar with brown bears,

---

20 An essay entitled 'Hypnagogia' by Caspar Henderson, reproduced in Barkham, P. (2021) *The Wild Isles: An Anthology of the Best British & Irish Nature Writing*. Head of Zeus, London. For a comprehensive review of early human history in Britain see Ashton, N. (2017) *Early Humans*. HarperCollins, London.

wolves and lynx, and perhaps even great beasts such as aurochs, cave lions and straight-tusked elephants. There was plenty going on in the British countryside in those days, despite our absence – in part, *because* of our absence.

Humans eventually returned, though we retreated again during spells when the climate deteriorated. Only from about 12,000 years ago has Britain been continuously occupied by people, and that's when things really began to change. Forests were cleared, land was settled, and some of the larger mammals and birds were hunted to extinction. From that time onwards, wild animals have known what a person is, and what to do when one comes too close.

Once I leave the wood, the game is up. No view is free from the marks of human endeavour. In the glen below, looking back towards the house, I see fields with dykes, farm buildings, fences and domestic livestock. In the hill country ahead of me, the slopes are blanketed with alien conifers, draped over the hills in straight-edged shapes, leaving no doubt as to their unnatural history.

* * *

The ash woods are full of native species that have been with us for thousands of years. Now I'm up in the hills, though, things are very different. There are native plants here too – but they have been squeezed hard by plants that are only here because of humans.

Introduced species get a bad press. Yet there is a view that we should learn to be a little more relaxed about them. Almost everyone accepts that some species cause trouble and need to be managed – rats on important seabird islands, Japanese knotweed outcompeting native wildflowers, and rhododendrons covering hillsides to the exclusion of the natural vegetation, for example.[21] But, so the argument goes, other

---

[21] All are local examples. The rats on Hestan Island must reduce the chances that seabirds other than gulls and cormorants will settle there to breed. I've found isolated clumps of Japanese knotweed along the burn and in the local hedgerows, where it looks innocuous enough, but if it spreads more widely it could begin to cause problems. Rhododendrons, too, are restricted to small areas not far from the village. From a distance, the blanket of pink flowers in early summer provides an ominous, if undoubtedly eye-catching, reminder of how good this plant is at excluding other species.

species end up fitting into their new environment, adding variety and helping, rather than hindering, the native wildlife. These places are certainly changed; they are no longer 'natural'. Most conservationists see that as a problem. But should we worry less about such things and focus more on getting the best out of these altered landscapes? Environmental journalist Fred Pearce certainly thinks so. He wrote a book called *The New Wild*, making his views crystal clear in the subtitle: 'Why Invasive Species will be Nature's Salvation'.[22] Academic and ecologist Chris Thomas thinks along similar lines:

> The default stance of conservation is to keep things as unchanged as possible or, alternatively, to return conditions to what they used to be, or somehow to make the Earth 'more natural' [...] Where is the logic in this? Attempting to prevent the establishment of 'alien' arrivals ... so as to maintain our ecosystems and species in some idealised state is not possible, nor is it obvious that the past state of the world is objectively preferable to the new state that is coming into existence.[23]

There is a lot to think about there, and the gently sloping hillside I've arrived at now is a good place to start. It's a large area, entirely surrounded by a 6-foot-high deer fence. There have been other token efforts locally to restore native trees to small areas, involving ranks of plastic tubes to guard hand-planted saplings. But it's only here, protected within the fence, that trees have been able to re-establish naturally over a large area. I can only guess at the history. I suspect the intention was to encourage yet more conifers to grow – in this case, through a process of natural regeneration within the fenced area rather than the usual hand-planting of individual trees. But, whatever the objectives, conifers are far from dominant inside the fence.

---

22 Pearce, F. (2015) *The New Wild: Why Invasive Species will be Nature's Salvation*. Beacon Press, Boston.
23 Thomas, C. (2017) *Inheritors of the Earth: How Nature is Thriving in an Age of Extinction*. Allen Lane, Milton Keynes.

Entry is by sliding aside a large square panel in one corner. No-one has been here for a while (perhaps since it was first installed) so it takes a few seconds to work the base of the panel free from its embrace of grasses. As I pull it firmly back into place I catch myself looking around for deer, half-thinking they might be watching, trying to work out how to get in.

It's a good-sized area of perhaps a quarter of a square kilometre. It's big enough and the trees are high enough for it to be easy to lose your bearings. And that's no bad thing. The recovering forest feels wild. The vegetation is self-willed, governed by chance events and natural processes rather than the whims of people. But it's far from natural; the mix of trees here could never have occurred without humans. Self-sown Sitka spruce and Douglas firs have moved in from the surrounding plantations. They mix with non-native sycamores (from eastern Europe), as well as a whole suite of native trees including birches, willows, rowan and alder. Some areas are so thick and tangled with vegetation that they are all but impenetrable to humans. (This is sometimes cited as a drawback to natural regeneration, but when there is so much concern about human disturbance to wildlife, perhaps it is an advantage.) There are also plenty of open areas that are easier to walk through, with the trees more widely spaced, and heather, tussocks of grass and bracken covering the ground.

I love the fact that this area is not moulded by the ideas of humans. But it's difficult to get used to the strange mix of species. One thing is clear: with the possible exception of the ash woods I walked through earlier, nowhere else close to home supports as many breeding birds. There are garden warblers singing from the scrubby areas, incongruously flying between willows and young Sitka spruce trees. Other warblers include whitethroats, blackcaps and chiffchaffs as well as the ubiquitous willow warblers. Tree pipits are singing from more open areas, and a male cuckoo is clearly in it for the long haul in trying to attract a mate, singing non-stop. He has competition because another bird starts up, inserting each of his double notes into the gaps left by the first. Presumably this is deliberate; both birds wish to be heard and are interested in listening to the competition. One of them may be in luck, because a little later I hear the lovely bubbling call of a female.

Wild flowers are doing well here, including some of the species at home in the ash woods. There are bluebells, primroses and violets, and in the damper places the lovely nodding heads of water avens and rosettes of insectivorous common butterworts, yet to send up their flower stalks.

Badgers have pushed their way under the fence, and I'm able to follow one of their paths for a while; a welcome strip of level ground through the heather, handily skirting the boggiest terrain. I find evidence that deer have tried to gain entry in the form of a detached roe deer leg snagged on the fence where it has been damaged by a fallen tree. The animal must have been caught as it jumped from one side to the other in the only place that was low enough to try. Subsequently the hill foxes, and perhaps badgers too, must have scavenged everything that could be pulled free, leaving the leg dangling pathetically from the top wire. Other deer, I see now, have been more successful. There are droppings, and hoof slots have been pressed into the mud. Soon, I hear a deer barking from somewhere unseen within the scrub. This is probably no bad thing. The trees are now so well established that browsing in moderation will result in a mix of dense vegetation and more open areas, helping to maintain a diversity of wildlife.

One of the reasons I love the old ash woods is that they look the same, and support the same species, as they have done for thousands of years. In a world that we have altered so radically, there seems to be something special about that – something worth hanging onto. It's undeniably true that humans are just as much a part of nature as every other species, but because we have come to dominate the planet, that's not a particularly helpful way to think about conservation. A conifer plantation, or the deer-fenced land I'm walking through now, or even a concrete urban jungle, may be just as 'natural' as an ancient woodland in a technical sense. But I can't feel the same way about any of them as I do about the ash woods. This hillside, though, despite the fingerprints of humanity, is a notch above the vast plantations. Nature – or, if you prefer, *non-human* nature – has been allowed more of a free rein here inside the fence, and that adds value to this place, despite its eclectic mix of tree species. I'm very glad it's here.

The new wild

* * *

Humans were making a living from these hills long before the plantations came. I'm now back outside the deer fence, following another animal barrier: one of the old stone dykes that runs through endless lines of young spruce trees. It was built to contain livestock when this whole area was grazing land. Now redundant, it provides a handy route through the forest. The trees here have been felled and replanted. Counting the rings on one of the stumps reveals it was cut when it was 35 years old.

To escape the conifers for a while I'm heading to a place with much older reminders of human occupation: the ancient hill fort of Dungarry. It's well off the beaten track. No one ever comes here, but the ruins have spared the hill it rests on from the trees. The conifers creep up the lower slopes but higher up, near the ruins, planting was presumably not allowed. Hawthorn bushes dot the flanks and in the open areas, grasses, heather and bluebells vie for dominance. The bluebells do best in the damper gullies, thickening into hazy patches here and there, then narrowing into veins that wind up towards the summit. I follow one to the top.

The remains are not much to look at. Just a rectangle about the size of a tennis court, outlined by lines of ancient stones covered in lichen and in parts a thick layer of moss. But it's easy to connect to deep time here. The place feels old. It is referred to locally as Roman, but according to what I can find online it has never been dated: the archaeological work simply hasn't been done, and the element of mystery only adds to its appeal.[24]

Humans leave traces everywhere. Our towns have old buildings and walls, often going back to Roman times. But out here, the structures left behind by people are somehow more arresting. I think it's because they have been left to decay at their own pace, and no newer structures have been built to supersede them. As inside the deer fence, natural processes have been allowed to do their work, albeit over a far longer timescale. Perhaps it's also because there is no one left in these hills.

---

24 The following resource has a searchable map together with summary information for all of Britain and Ireland's recorded hillforts: Atlas of Hillforts (https://hillforts.arch.ox.ac.uk).

Places once busy with people and the fortifications necessary to protect them are now empty and silent, opening up space for contemplation.

As I'm sitting on the biggest pile of stones a red kite drifts across, offering another strand of connection to the past. When this place was a focal point for human activity, red kites would have been here too, making the most of the feeding opportunities that humans and their livestock inevitably provide. The kites were missing for a while. Now they are back, though there is little of interest for them up here these days.

* * *

Today's walk, with only birdsong for company, has reminded me of my own personal 'new wild'. My ability to hear birds is far short of what it once was. One ear barely functions other than to generate irritating sounds of its own. And while the other remains serviceable, it no longer registers the highest frequencies. A wren is singing now from the rubble of the fort. I'm only a few metres away and it's one of our loudest songsters, but when I listen carefully I realise I'm not hearing the whole song. Rather, I'm piecing it together from memory and the notes that remain audible; I know it so well that my brain is able to fill in (or at least recognise and account for) the gaps. That's something to be grateful for I suppose; at least it still sounds like a wren.

But how much am I missing out on? The deterioration has happened so gradually, over such a long time, I find that an impossible question to answer. The sounds of some birds, though, have gone from my world forever. I'll never again hear the calls of redwings on a still autumn night as they fly over to spend another winter with us. (Only when they appear in the hedgerows will I know they have returned.) I'll never hear another singing goldcrest or treecreeper or spotted flycatcher, and it's remarkable how that cuts down on the opportunities for seeing them. The plantations I've walked through today might have been full of goldcrests, a bird that thrives in conifers. But they are tiny, unobtrusive, foliage-coloured birds; without the sounds, I'm none the wiser.

My sight is still good, though my eyes have developed a mess of the dark spots and lines that my optician referred to as floaters. She suggested acceptance and stoicism as the best way forward: 'They'll bother you less if you just try to ignore them.' It's good advice. Occasionally, though, when I'm following a distant bird in flight, it's easier said than done: *Is that the bird, or just one of the spots within my eyes?* Follow the wrong one for a split second and by the time I realise, the real thing has slipped away.

My ears and eyes have been known to work together to conspire against me. Lying in bed one night, dulled by tiredness, I heard the familiar high-pitched whine of a mosquito. On went the light; I knew I'd have to kill it before sleep would come again. And yes, there it was – a fuzzy dark shape floating in front of my face. I clapped my hands together to squash it, only then realising the mistake.

* * *

The light is starting to go. Even down back at the house I love the way the onset of darkness changes the feel of the place. The slopes of Bengairn gradually disappear, and the few buildings we can make out from the kitchen window are erased from view. The effect is more powerful still when there is low cloud or fog. Then even the few distant lights towards the edge of the village disappear. Isolation settles over the house. More is left to the imagination, and the connection with all the wilder elements of our world becomes stronger.

Out here the effect is intensified. Surrounded by hills as I am, there are no lights to erase. There is no moon, and almost certainly no other people for miles in all directions. The blackness is just what I need for the glow-worms (though, sadly, they do not give themselves up tonight) but it feels strangely unsettling. Perhaps it's because I've been thinking about the long human history of the place; somewhere now remote and eerily silent would once have supported a thriving community. Go back far enough and there would have been serious predators of humans here too. I'm not superstitious or religious, so I shouldn't be worried about ghosts, and I know full well that the predators are long gone. But logic is irrelevant. The fear is innate and inescapable. We crave contentment, and we easily forget that we are survival machines, built not for comfort and relaxation but to ensure that we pre-empt and dodge threats. Doing this requires constant vigilance, or at least it did in our not-too-distant past. Is that movement in the vegetation a snake? Is that the sound of footsteps approaching? Is that shape through the trees a predator waiting for its chance? We have the potential for long lives. It's better to be overly cautious and wrong a thousand times than to miss a real threat just once. Individuals who adopted a more relaxed approach may have lived happier lives (for a while), but they have been weeded out by their rare, yet inevitable, misjudgements.

There is nothing for me to fear out here in the new wild. But unshakeable instincts offer a reminder of our long, eventful history; a connection to an old wild that has gone forever but lives on in our minds.

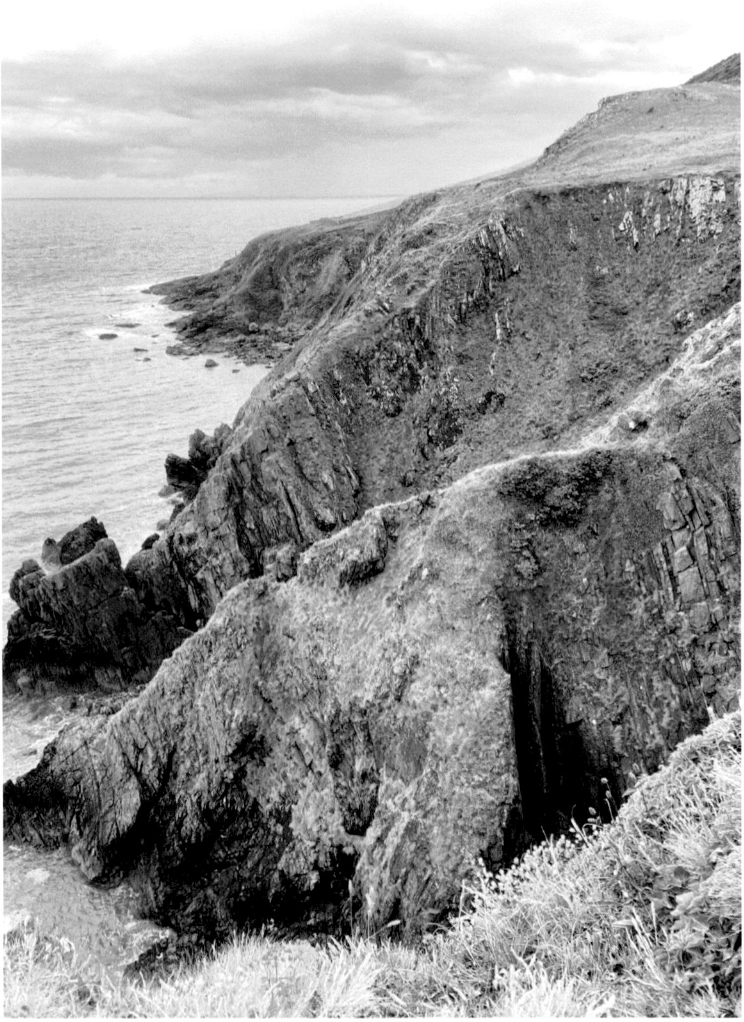

8

The land's edge

The cliffs at the foot of the glen; a place for breeding seabirds, and the Solway's special wintering birds.

A day spent looking away from land starts with a 90-minute trudge across it. Spring is slowly taking over from winter, and this is one of the first pleasantly warm days of the year. I follow the farm track that runs by the house, then the narrow lane down through the village, before turning right onto the coast road to the Balcary Bay Hotel. From here, it's uphill through sheep fields as the cliffs rise up from the bay. Walking along a coastline doubles the bird interest. There are the typical birds of the fields and small woods that flank the cliffs. But away to my left there is nothing but the open waters of the Solway. The more adaptable of the gulls blur these boundaries, drifting casually between land and ocean. But for many seabirds there is no such compromise; the only acknowledgement that land exists is now, in the breeding season, when they need somewhere dry to rest their eggs. To see petrels, auks and the more discerning of the gulls, you must come down to the shore.

The cliffs run for about a mile from Balcary Point to Airds Point, served by a narrow footpath that winds precariously along the top. The rock face is almost vertical in places, and the ill-formed path cuts into it perilously close to the edge. There are lots of little inlets and a series of caves down at sea level. It's appealing to the human eye and already I can see (and hear) that seabirds appreciate it too; here are innumerable ledges, crevices and caverns that ground predators will struggle to reach.

* * *

The waters are placid today, but this is a dramatic place to spend time when a winter storm blows in, especially if the wind is between the south and east. It drives the sea into the rocks, churning up foam that is hurled up and over the 70-metre cliffs and away inland. Who knows where it might end up? Even balls of whelk egg-cases are carried up from the shore below and left to roll and bounce their way along the footpath. These conditions present genuine dangers for the unwary. Back in the early 1990s, a few days before Christmas, two friends were fishing from rocks at the base of these cliffs. Both were caught out by a large wave and washed into the sea; only one was able to scramble back to safety.

When the winter seas are calmer, Balcary Point provides an excellent vantage point, offering views out over Auchencairn Bay and across to Hestan Island. On an overcast day or in the afternoon when the sun has moved around to the west – and so glare is less of a problem – this is the best place locally to catch up with two Solway specialities. Both are seaducks, and both need places where shellfish and other sedentary marine creatures are abundant, and where the water is shallow enough for them to be reached.

Common scoters look black from a distance but when closer to shore the brown, pale-cheeked females can be picked out easily from the darker males. Closer still, and that lovely flash of yellow on the bill of the males is visible. A sweep of the telescope usually reveals loose, scattered flocks, most of them way out across the water – specks of black, like flies swarming unevenly across a surface. On my first few visits I tried to count them. But even a slight swell hides the more distant birds, and groups are constantly flying this way and that, moving into areas already counted and away from places I have yet to scan. At any moment, an unknowable proportion of the birds is either underwater, behind a wave, or out of sight across the vastness of the firth. It's hopeless. So now I jot down 'hundreds' or, more typically, 'thousands' in my notebook. And instead of counting, I focus the telescope on the group closest to the shore and watch for a while. Flock members bob buoyantly on the surface of the sea, resting, perhaps preening, the males chasing each other to impress nearby females, and when the tide (and mood) is right, diving down into the murky, silt-laden waters.

In days gone by bird trappers would fix loose nets into the mud exposed at low tide further east along the coast from here.[25] Covered by the sea as the tide rose, the nets would entangle the scoters diving to reach food in the substrate below, and they would drown, to be retrieved by the trappers on the next falling tide. Apparently, hundreds could be caught this way, providing welcome sustenance (or income) for local people.

If the sea is calm, the light good, the scoters not too far offshore and (most importantly) if I'm in the right frame of mind, there's a game to be played here. It involves scanning carefully through the flocks, bird by bird, looking for an individual that is a little bigger, with pale smudges on the face and, if it chooses to cooperate, a thin line of white in the otherwise dark, folded wings. These are velvet scoter. They aren't aways here, and when they do turn up they are outnumbered, thousands to one, by their abundant cousins. On most visits I don't find them. But every so often I'll get lucky, and manage to pick out a bird or two from the masses. Occasionally they spoil the game by taking flight. Now, even at a distance, the gleaming white wing-panels shine out from the otherwise dark body and wings.

The scaup is the other special seaduck here. It is far less abundant than the scoters, but groups of up to 40 or so – always a mix of males and brown, white-faced females – can sometimes be found here in winter. The pale flanks of the males catch the light, even on the dullest days, making them easy to pick out, and if they are close enough and the light is good, that wonderful tinge of green on the head is shown off to full effect.

Fish-eating birds also winter here, vanishing from view as soon as they slip down under the surface. Cormorants are common, and I usually find a few red-throated divers, narrow bills angled up above the horizontal. How they catch fish in the sludgy waters of the Solway is anyone's guess, though perhaps poor visibility works in their favour.

---

25 Young, J.G. (1999) 'Bird-netting: some historical aspects.' Lecture notes for the 25th Scottish Ringing Conference, Braemar.

Fish must struggle to see them coming, and so short-range ambushes might be highly effective. Whatever the method, it works. Cormorants often pop up to the surface with a fish, and I'll watch the prey squirming frantically for its last few seconds before it disappears inside the bird.

Large gulls lack the ability to dive deeply, so they use other techniques to get fish. Great black-backed gulls sit patiently – menacingly – on the sea, deliberately taking up station close to a fishing cormorant. They are hoping a large fish will be brought to the surface; one that will take time to handle, opening up an opportunity for them to fly in and steal it. The cormorants know the game, but there's not much they can do about it. If they expend energy moving to a new, and perhaps less productive, fishing spot, the gull will follow.

Gulls keep an eye on each other as well as on other birds, and we've all seen the chaotic chases that result from one of them finding food only for others to insist on a share. One time, I was distracted from the activity offshore by a herring gull with a starfish on the rocks below me. It was soon forced to drop its catch by three vigorous pursuers. The food was picked up by one of the chasing birds, which instantly became the target of a renewed pursuit. A winner was finally declared when the pursuers simply gave up, as if tired from the game. I suspect it's the hungriest bird that has the strongest motivation to outlast its challengers, which I suppose is a sensible way to settle things.

* * *

But back to the here and now. It's a few days from the end of April and winter feels a long way behind us. There are no crashing waves, nor any flying foam balls to dodge, and most of the seaducks have already moved north towards their breeding grounds.

I find a good place to settle down with the telescope. My chosen spot is sheltered from the breeze, on a downslope to one side of a small headland, with a good view along the line of the cliffs as well as out to sea. I'm high enough that I'll be able to pick out seabirds well offshore that would otherwise be hidden by the swell.

I do this a lot; I sit in the same spot and wait to see what comes by. It works well enough in any landscape, though inside the woods or up in the hills it can be a while before anything interesting happens. Seascapes are different; here, the theme is constant change. Tides ebb and flow. Zooplankton and small fish respond unpredictably, keeping the birds guessing. Seabirds are always on the move and when commuting from one place to another often fly close to shore; it provides a clearly defined line to follow, and close to land there is more shelter from the wind. Headlands are the best places of all; seabirds travelling from one side to the other keep their journey as short as possible by passing close to the tip.

At first, though, it's landbirds that grab my attention. The cliffs are a mix of bare rock and impenetrable tangles of vegetation clinging to even the steepest slopes. The sheep are unable to graze here, and ivy, blackthorn and brambles have taken advantage. The bushes are regularly battered by strong onshore winds and drenched in salt spray; they are contorted and hug the surface, but they have, nevertheless, managed to smother sizeable areas. And birds normally found in woodland and scrub are using them. I spend a few minutes watching a pair of robins that have set up home in this strange, near-vertical landscape. As they forage, they necessarily fly 'up' and 'down' as well as along the face of the cliff; the size of their territory, if measured horizontally in the usual way, would scarcely register. They must have young, as I see one of the adults carrying a bright white faecal sac to dispose of away from the nest. It seems a terrifying location in which to breed – but if you can fly, then of course it's not a problem. And the increased security against predatory mammals is no doubt very welcome.

Jackdaws, too, are using dense patches of ivy. They cruise along the cliffs, and every so often a bird draws in its wings and shoots itself into a tiny gap in the foliage. There must be, behind the vegetation, ledges or crevices in the rocks that provide nesting sites.

There is another songbird here: the rock pipit. It uses the full extent of the cliffs, from the short, sheep-nibbled grass on the tops to the beach far below, and it stays year-round. The seabirds come to tend their eggs, and most of the landbirds use this place for nesting or drop in periodically as visitors from other habitats. For the rock pipit, though, this thin line where the sea meets the land is a permanent home.

Just as seabirds sometimes pass close to shore when travelling from one place to another, so too do migrating landbirds. Having travelled across the ocean, they often then follow the coast, which provides an obvious navigational line, before they branch off inland towards their breeding sites. Today there is not much activity, but every so often a few swallows sweep gracefully by, pushing east, using updrafts of air from a sea breeze flowing up and over the cliffs.

There's a lull in activity before a peregrine breaks the spell. It hurtles along the cliffs, and I barely have time to register it before it turns 90 degrees and swings away inland to try its luck there. I see this bird inland as well, but there's something special about watching it here; it is often at eye level, its powerful, thick-set outline set off perfectly against the drama of the cliffs. There will be a nest on a cliff ledge somewhere, and birds from a varied 'surf-and-turf' menu will keep the young well fed.

* * *

But the landbirds are a side show. All around this small headland, birds that spend much of their lives out of sight of land are at their nest sites. Herring gulls, lesser black-backs and fulmars have sought out little flat patches of grass among the jumble of rock and steeper ground. On sheer rock faces, mostly hidden from view, are the kittiwakes, nervous and skittish, spilling out over the sea every so often before they agree among themselves that it's safe after all, and drift back to their ledges.

Guillemots are packed tightly together on the lower parts of the cliffs, while razorbills are dotted about at individual nest sites, well separated from others of their own kind; two very different breeding strategies from otherwise similar birds. Different shades of black and white are key, both to finding the auks' nest sites and then distinguishing between the two species. Occupied ledges are liberally splashed with whitewash and stand out from the bare rock. Homing in on the birds, the razorbills are given away by their jet-black plumage, perfectly setting off the brilliant white lines on the bill. Guillemots are duller, with a browner tinge. The difference is obvious when a direct comparison is possible, even in flight. I watch now as a group of nine auks comes whirring in towards the cliffs, skimming the surface of the

The land's edge

sea. While they are still 500 metres away, I can see that there are seven guillemots, with two, darker, razorbills tucked in at the back. They often fly in mixed groups, both species keen to maximise the benefits of safety in numbers as they commute to and from their ledges.

I have a good view into the wide mouth of a cave just above the beach. Rock doves are swooping in and out. They look like the wild-type birds, with two thick black stripes on uniform grey wings and striking white rumps, though genetic studies have shown that in southern Scotland the birds have widely interbred with feral pigeons. On a previous visit to these cliffs, I found direct evidence of this mixing: the leg of a predated racing pigeon, complete with the closed ring (fitted when it was a chick) that confirmed its captive origin. Racing was its thing, but it had met something faster.

I'm delighted to see a pair of black guillemots. They too fly inside the cave, before landing on a rock a few metres from the entrance. Here, out of the light, their dark bodies disappear, leaving the white half-moons on the wings and their bright red legs apparently floating in space. Later, I watch a pair just offshore. They are sitting on the water but fly up every so often to execute low, fast circuits over the sea, no doubt strengthening the bond between them. They are like a pair of fighter jets performing a precision synchronised display, banking sharply at just the same moment, wings almost touching, and showing off the black-and-white plumage to full effect as they race around above the water.

It's a stroke of good fortune for me that our glen is flanked by these cliffs. For the fulmars, kittiwakes and the three auks, the Solway to the east of here lacks suitable breeding places; this is as far inside the firth as they come when looking for a place to rest their eggs.

* * *

The hours drift by and as well as enjoying the birds, I'm relishing the absence of anthropogenic sounds. There is no one else here, and the gentle lapping of wave against rock helps block out more distant noises – the odd jumbo perhaps – that might otherwise intrude. That leaves seabirds to dominate the soundscape. There is the familiar seaside backdrop of herring gulls. And rising up from below on the breeze come the strange, guttural cries of fulmars and guillemots, either pair-bonding or squabbling, or a little of both. The kittiwakes are silent for a while, and then all shout their name at once, as those on the ledges welcome new arrivals from the sea. The most spirited, if incongruous, contribution comes from above the cliffs: a lone red-legged partridge is sitting on a low stone dyke, firing explosive bursts of its rasping, mechanical song into the breeze. Jackdaws chip in with excitable metallic 'kya's whenever a group happens by, and there is an occasional deep 'gronk' from a raven as it glides past, wings stiff as it works the wind.

The breeze stirs together the smells of land and sea, as well as the sounds, as unpredictable eddies of air swirl about the cliffs. The tang of salt is never far away. But when the wind is just right it is replaced by the stench of seabird droppings wafting up from the ledges below. Then, every so often, the familiar sweet scent of coconut drifts down in the other direction from above the clifftop. Each time, it's enough to make me turn from the sea and look back at the dense masses of gorse, blazing with a million yellow flowers. I remember I have the long walk home, and start to thread my way through the bushes and back down to the lane. I'll return later in the season, by which time, I hope, eggs will have become young.

* * *

Two weeks have slipped by since the longest day of the year, and many more since my last visit here. The cliffs are a lengthy trudge from home, so it has been all too easy to postpone my return. But if I want to watch young guillemots and razorbills balancing precariously on their ledges, there is no delaying it any longer.

Early July might feel like the start of peak summer for us humans, but for many birds summer's main task is already drawing to a close. For the songbirds that rear a single brood, this is a time to wind down after the frenetic activity of previous weeks; their young have fledged and are finding their own way in the world. There are still a few cuckoos about, but some of them are already on their way south, moving back towards their wintering grounds; the mating duties of the males finished a few weeks earlier, and soon after mating the females would have left their eggs in the unwitting care of others. So for the cuckoos there is no reason to linger.

Other birds are still hard at it, though. Plenty of songbirds see their young safely to independence only to start all over again with a second, perhaps a third, and even a fourth brood. Larger birds, including wildfowl and birds of prey, have just the one brood, but the eggs take weeks to hatch, and the young must be looked after for several more weeks, so the breeding season is protracted. Seabirds, too, have a long breeding season. And if I've judged things well, activity along the cliffs will be peaking just about now.

It is quickly apparent that things have moved on since I was last here. The sights, sounds and smells all tell the same story – there are *more* of all of them. The distinctive stench of breeding seabirds – the result of weeks of accumulated guano decaying into the air – is now almost overpowering whenever it wafts up from below. You wouldn't call it pleasant, but I don't mind it; it's the unmistakable smell of a seabird colony, and a seabird colony is never a bad place to spend time.

A lot of the breeding ledges are on sheer cliffs facing directly out to sea, so are hidden from view from above. But there are a few places, on little promontories close to the cliff edge, where parts of the colony can be seen. A stack of rock just offshore holds a few nests, viewable only by crawling out to the edge of the cliffs and lying full length, head poking out above the abyss. I manage about two minutes before unease overwhelms curiosity, but it's enough to see a well-grown razorbill chick, sheltering between an adult and the rock face behind it. And there are several kittiwakes, still sitting tight on eggs or small chicks. The stack is a perfect breeding place – a miniature island. It has good ledges on its vertical walls, and is surrounded by sea on all sides, so the nest sites are beyond the reach of even the most determined ground predators. Herring gulls, too, are using it, their nests of dead grass built on the well-vegetated green roof that caps the bare rock.

On the main cliffs, razorbills are dotted about here and there, favouring splendid isolation from others of their own kind. Guillemots are patchily distributed, too, but that's where the similarity ends; rather than breeding alone, they cluster together in small but densely packed groups. This is an important part of their defence strategy; if a large gull flies over, looking for an egg or chick to steal, it will be met with an array of long, sharp beaks jabbing up threateningly towards the sky.

The often made comparison between auks and penguins is understandable. They are not closely related but fulfil much the same roles in their respective hemispheres, so it's hardly surprising they have evolved to look similar. I find it more surprising that they make similar sounds. The guillemots I can hear now, squabbling with their neighbours, remind me so much of emperor penguins that I half-expect Morgan Freeman to pop up and provide a running commentary. One difference is that the auks have retained the power of flight. Penguins walk and swim to their feeding grounds: auks fly there. The sadly departed great auk, the razorbill's closest relative, no less, was flightless. And in the north Atlantic, a place that came to be dominated by humans, that was what sealed its fate.[26]

Guillemots and razorbills have their differences, but they share one aspect of breeding; throughout the long summer season, instant failure is only ever a few centimetres away. They use narrow ledges of bare rock or earth, with what looks like an unsurvivable drop to the sea below. Once laid, the single egg must not be allowed to roll. Once hatched, the chick is one careless step away from certain death. Movement is restricted to cautious shuffling, and I notice that the attending adults often stand between their chick and the lip of the ledge.

Kittiwake chicks face the same peril, and they too are programmed to keep movement to a minimum. Unlike the auks, they at least have a nest, with a shallow, concave cup, to reduce the risk of accidents. While the auks lay a single egg, kittiwakes usually lay two, and sometimes three, so space in the small nest quickly fills up. Young herring gulls have more freedom; the chicks are semi-precocial and begin to explore the area around their nest when only two or three days old. I watch one now on top of the stack – a robust, speckled ball of down, tottering

---

[26] Auks and penguins are linked by language too. 'Penguin' was once used for the great auk. The etymology is debated, but the word is plausibly derived from the Welsh *pen gwyn* meaning 'white head', a reference to the distinctive white patches in front of each eye. It seems that when explorers of the southern seas first saw penguins, they noticed the similar appearance, and named them accordingly.

about among the grasses. It mewls insistently at a nearby adult that I presume, at first, to be a parent – but it remains stoically unmoved, and the chick continues on its way.

* * *

I watch birds leaving the cliffs and wonder how far they will go. The two common auks make up the bulk of the numbers but there are also black guillemots, fulmars, kittiwakes, and lesser black-backed and herring gulls. Black guillemots are bottom feeders and rely on shallow water close into the shore; they won't go far. But the other birds are capable of much longer trips. If good feeding spots are hard to come by, they will fly many miles to seek them out.

Gulls and fulmars swallow food and regurgitate it when feeding their young. It's a handy adaptation, allowing them to take advantage of rich feeding grounds far from the colony. Even small items can be ingested and later fed to the chicks, transported back to the colony in the most efficient way possible. The auks, however, lack this ability; everything that their chicks eat must be carried back to land one beak-load at a time.

There are no puffins here, sadly – a bird whose fish-carrying apparatus outguns all its rivals. The colourful, notched beaks allow dozens of sandeels to be brought back to land, each one wedged carefully at right angles between the two mandibles. Razorbills too can carry up to about 20 small fish at a time. But the two guillemot species, with their narrow, pointed beaks, seem doubly hindered. Not only must they carry fish back to shore (rather than swallowing them for regurgitation), but they can take only one at a time. It seems an unnecessary constraint. What if only small fish are abundant? A razorbill's beakful will still make a worthwhile meal, but the guillemot is limited to a single fish. And yet, this is the commonest auk on the cliffs here, and in Britain as a whole. What, I wonder, is its secret?

A series of grating shrieks carry over the background noise of seabirds. I locate the source and follow its progress as it flaps powerfully along the cliffs towards me. I've still not worked out where the peregrines are nesting. My guess is that, like many of the seabirds, they have chosen a rocky ledge out of sight from the clifftop. But this lone fledgling, already flying well, shows that they have had a successful season. It drops down onto the turf, landing on a small rock among fading sea pinks and yellow spikes of lady's bedstraw, no more than 50 metres away. A disgruntled rock pipit buzzes, fly-like, around it. Ignored, and with no safe way of escalating the protest, it soon gives up. Red-and-black burnet moths and meadow brown butterflies – creatures of high summer – jink above the turf between me and the peregrine. And I fancy I see the young bird watching one of the butterflies as it passes, jerking its head to keep one eye on the target as it drifts by.

A few weeks later, on a return visit, I'll hear the same distinctive calls before I've even turned onto the footpath from the lane by the hotel. And I'll look up instinctively just in time to see two peregrines come together in the air as a small package is passed deftly from one to the other. The birds are too high to make out plumage details, but this, I'm sure, is an adult passing food to one of its youngsters, simultaneously providing sustenance and a lesson in handling prey.

* * *

Today there is plenty of activity along the cliffs, but a lot is happening offshore too. Resources in the ocean are patchy and fluid. Endless tracts of water are all but empty. And then, suddenly, there is a place where food becomes abundant and accessible – perhaps a shoal of small fish pushed up to the surface by predatory fish (or something bigger) beneath them. It may not last long, so birds must take advantage while they can, homing in from all directions. These mixed-species gatherings are impossible to predict, so you have as much chance of seeing one by waiting patiently in the same spot as by taking a long walk along the coast. That's what I have in mind for the next few hours.

As always, my first scan of the sea comes with the hope of tell-tale splashes of white, combined with glimpses of dark fins. The Solway's harbour porpoises often reveal themselves this way when I spend time here. Earlier in the summer, I watched several larger animals with taller, gracefully recurved, dorsal fins and a more demonstrative demeanour;

they were bottle-nosed dolphins, close into the cliffs, adding vitality to the seascape in the way that only dolphins can.

Today, there are no dolphins – or porpoises for that matter. But there are thousands of little black dots, packed tightly together in several groups, out towards the wind farm. They are another sign that while here on the cliffs the breeding season is in full swing, for other birds it is already over. These common scoters are probably preparing for their annual moult, when they will drop all their main feathers simultaneously and become flightless for a few weeks. The males' contribution to breeding is minimal. At their breeding grounds on the tundra and heathland, far to the north, each of them pairs up, mates with a female – and, well, that's about it, really. Little wonder they have flown south already. The females that have returned here so soon are probably failed breeders with nothing left to hold them to the nesting areas.

A few gannets drift by. They might be from the colony on the small island of Scare (or Scar) Rocks off the tip of the Mull of Galloway, 40 miles to the west, though non-breeders or birds from the more distant (but much larger) colony on Ailsa Craig also wander into the Solway. They eye the waters below, and I wait, hopefully, for the moment of magic when one will furl itself into a dart and plunge, beak-first, onto an unsuspecting fish. (They are so adept at this that when coming in to land on the sea they adopt a similar behaviour; they glide in at a shallow angle, neck outstretched, and land head, rather than feet, first.)

The Sandwich tern is another bird that ranges over large areas of sea. Like the gannet, it doesn't breed locally, but I see them regularly enough from March onwards, through the summer. It has been called a super-tern because while smaller species stay close to their colony, Sandwich terns will travel over 30 miles to seek out food-rich hotspots. They dive from high above the surface, becoming fully submerged, much like the gannet, and can carry fish up to 25 centimetres long back to their young. When I walked by earlier there were five perched on the poles of the old salmon nets in the bay near the hotel, perhaps waiting for the fishing to improve, or maybe digesting a meal. Now, as three birds pass by, well offshore, I track their progress for a while, hoping they might reveal where the fish are.

A seabird feeding frenzy is a spectacle that is hard to beat. When I carried out seabird surveys for the old Nature Conservancy Council, our boat would occasionally pass through the middle of one, revealing the full, chaotic extent of the activity as hundreds of birds all tried to grab their share.[27] The problem for small shoaling bait fish is given away by the name – everything else wants to eat them. They are pursued from below by larger fish, and sometimes mammals, and from above by an array of seabirds, all with slightly different techniques. The auks swim after them using wings for propulsion. Shags have a similar approach but use webbed feet to generate speed, and their long necks to reach out in front of them. Terns and gannets plunge down from above; the fish is caught before it is even aware of the threat. If the attacks become intense, bait fish will break the surface of the sea, flinging themselves into the air as a last, desperate attempt to escape. For a few moments the protagonists exchange domains; the guillemots and razorbills are swimming beneath the surface of the water, while their prey are 'flying' through the air above. On a boat trip in Madeira, I witnessed the flying fish that have honed this behaviour to perfection. Mistaking our vessel for a threat as it approached, they broke the surface at speed, fins fanning out to become wings, enabling them to glide perhaps 10 metres or more before slipping back into the water, well out of harm's way.

But it's not happening here today. Not for the first time I wonder if the churned, sludgy waters of the Solway are far from ideal for these seabirds, which hunt fish primarily by sight. The birds I track as they fly from the cliffs seem to be heading well offshore, and will perhaps leave the Solway for the rich waters of the Irish Sea, far off to the southwest.

Before heading home, I creep out again to the cliff edge for a final look at the sea stack. Both razorbill parents are present now, with their pint-sized chick. Razorbills pair for life, and in contrast to the scoters offshore, they share their breeding duties. Now, approaching the time when they will disperse once again into the vastness of the open sea,

---

[27] An account of my time surveying offshore seabirds for the Nature Conservancy Council's Seabirds at Sea Team is included in Carter, I. (2021) *Human, Nature*. Pelagic Publishing, Exeter.

they are reinforcing the bond between them. There are bouts of mutual preening, and then a display that involves rhythmic contortions of the neck, beaks gaping open. They are so immaculately uniformed in black and white that the bright yellow lining inside the bill seems strangely out of place; it's as if a little bit of each bird has somehow been painted the wrong colour.

Soon, one late evening, this young bird – and others like it – will leap into the space beyond its ledge. Barely half-grown and unable to fly properly, wings whirring frantically, it will hopefully splash down safely onto the sea below. At least one of its parents, but often only the male, will follow, landing close by. Together, they will swim away. I find the presence of all this new life as welcome as the returning migrants in spring. Both reveal things about the natural world that we don't normally experience directly. The arrival of swifts, swallows and the massed ranks of warblers shows that their wintering areas and migration routes hold food enough to see them through to spring. And here on the cliffs, these growing chicks confirm that – despite all the damage we have done – the adults can find sufficient food in our seas, not only to feed themselves, but to rear their fast-growing young. The world – this bit of it, for now – still works.

Most seabirds are long-lived. Some of the youngsters I've been watching today – those with luck on their side – will outlast me. If only we can look after them. I hope they will return to these cliffs as adults. And I hope they will continue to pull fish from the ocean, carrying them back to dry land to feed generations of seabirds to come.

***

There's a pleasant surprise on my walk home, when I'm almost back at the house. Finally, after 18 months of living here, a barn owl shows itself, skirting the edge of the field next to the ash woods. The reticence of this bird has been an increasing source of frustration for me, added to by regular reports from neighbours, the unmistakable calls after dark, and – worst of all – Hazel's gleeful sighting in broad daylight one day when I was away from home.

Now, watching it work the edge of the field, stalling briefly over possible targets before sweeping onwards, I think of the contrasts between this hunter and our other resident owl. Both are a similar size and, as I've found, can be tricky to see. And both make their living from small mammals. But that's where the similarities end. One is finely patterned in brown to blend into its woodland habitat. It keeps mainly to cover, sitting patiently on a favoured branch, waiting for prey to appear within range. The other is a shock of white, capable of spooking country-dwellers walking home late in the day. It shuns the cover of the woods in favour of a restless patrolling of the open fields. The tawny owl produces the soft, mellow hoots with which we are all so familiar, while the barn owl is responsible for a range of unearthly shrieks and wails that only enhance its mysterious reputation. Both add their own individual magic to this place.

After a long day I close the back door. *The world – this bit of it, for now – still works.*

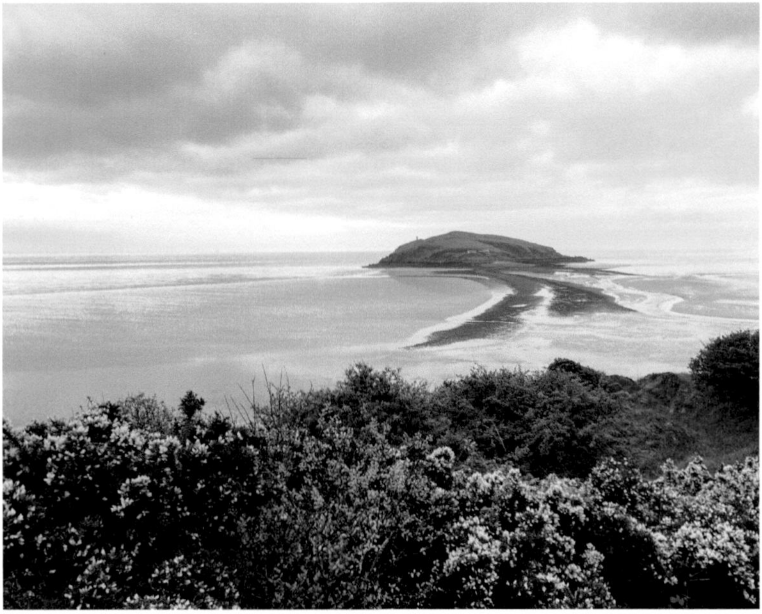

9

Island life

Almorness Point and a night offshore; alone with the gulls and a trio of special mammals.

Dotted white with sheep and gulls – and from a distance it's difficult to tell them apart – the rocky, green-topped mound of Hestan Island guards the entrance to the bay. It provides shelter from the wilder waters of the Solway beyond, and it lends a certain intimacy to our glen, a natural finishing point for the eye when looking down from the farm or the hill country above. With my love of islands, it feels odd for me not to have spent time there yet. But it's accessible only at low tide (and not every low tide) so to avoid having to dash there and back before the sea returns an overnight stay is required.[28] That's what I have in mind today. It's early May, the weather forecast is encouraging (if not entirely rain-free), and by late afternoon the sea will have fallen sufficiently low to expose the long natural causeway between Hestan and the mainland.

Beryl Scott and her husband lived in the remote cottage on Hestan Island for a few years in the 1950s, and she wrote a short book about their time as the island's only residents.[29] They grew vegetables, caught fish, tended the sheep and made sure that the small, unmanned

---

[28] On certain neap tides in the monthly cycle the tidal range is not sufficient to expose the causeway, and so the island can't be reached. Spring tides have a greater range; the sea reaches higher up the shore at high tide and falls further back when it recedes. Tide tables are generally reliable, but weather conditions, especially the wind strength and direction, and the atmospheric pressure, can have effects that override the predictions.

[29] Scott, Revd. B.M. (2003) *On a Galloway Island: Fulfilment of Dreams and a Spiritual Journey*. Privately published.

lighthouse didn't run out of fuel.[30] Remarkably, they also ran a small business making church organs, assembling the instruments in an outbuilding before dismantling them so they could be taken across to the mainland in their small boat and delivered to a local church.

Beryl Scott's book is the reason I've taken the car and come the long way around, despite having watched people cross to Hestan from Balcary, within walking distance of home. Her book tells how the Solway's strong currents are constantly reshaping the seabed, and even places with a covering of firm mud can be scoured by the sea, forming dangerous potholes down to the more treacherous, softer mud below. The book includes a horror story or two, of feet plunging through the surface layer to be gripped firmly by mud as the fast Solway tide rushes back in. So I'm taking no chances. The point at Almorness is a short drive and then a longish walk away, but from there at low tide the Hestan Rack stretches from the island almost the whole way across to the mainland. I'll have just one short stretch of grey, gloopy mud to navigate.

* * *

To reach the point and the causeway I have a walk of an hour or so from the lane. The estate here is heavily wooded, with mature oaks dominating the eastern side, and elsewhere a wonderful mix of regenerating woodland, scrub and lightly grazed flower-rich grassland. In the fine, calm weather it feels like peak spring. St Mark's flies are everywhere – two weeks later than advertised – legs dangling as they jink frenetically about in the air. And the bluebells are at their best. They cover the ground beneath the trees as well as the open areas, filling gaps between the bushes with a blue haze, studded white with stitchwort and the occasional albino bluebell. To complete the spring theme, a greylag mother leads a brood of fluffy, yellow goslings through the flowers, pushing quickly on when she notices me. The youngsters

---

30 The original lighthouse was built in 1893, and there is still a working light today, now powered by solar panels. Its distinctive pattern is two white flashes followed by a gap of ten seconds. Someone on the mainland (in Kippford, I think, from where it is visible) is tasked with checking it regularly and alerting the authorities if it stops working.

keep getting caught up among the stems, little wings beating frantically to push through obstructions as they struggle to keep up.

All the migrant birds have returned now, and I'm pleased to see a male redstart in one of the old parkland oaks by the farm, and further along the track my first garden warblers of the year, singing off against each other. It's a ritual of mine to try to find the first one I hear. That way I see at least one garden warbler each summer, and am reassured that I can still pick out the song from that of the similar blackcap. For once, the closest bird is in obliging mood, sitting out at the edge of the foliage as the notes pour out, 'shuttling up and down, like a rippling brook', as one of my field guides has it.

Nearby I hear what sounds like a red kite, and I spend a few moments trying to work out if it's the real thing or a blackbird or song thrush incorporating mimicry into its song. I'm still trying to work it out when the bird itself ends any doubts, flying up from a perch above the track. A long, barred primary falls away and twists down to the ground below, dislodged by the clatter of wings as the kite weaves its way through the trees. It is flying below the canopy, which is a good indication that there's a nest nearby. Scanning the trees, I find it: a mass of sticks lodged in a fork, close to the trunk.

At the tip of the peninsula I have an hour to wait before the tide falls sufficiently. So I backtrack a little to watch a pair of ringed plovers I passed earlier. They have chosen one of the point's small sand and shell beaches for their territory, and therein lies a problem. There's no-one around today, this early in the season, but that won't last; they have selected the very place that will draw in visitors. The firm white sand is easy on the eyes and the feet, and the shallow gradient down to the sea looks perfect for families with children to entertain or dogs to exercise. The long walk in from the road will limit numbers. But on a small beach such as this, it still might be too many.

Last summer, on Mull, I witnessed the difficulties these birds face. As an amorous couple walked along the top of the beach, the pair I'd been watching flew up and circled over them, calling incessantly, before settling on the sand lower down the beach. No reaction from the humans. Next came tail-dragging, and then the broken-wing display as one of the pair fluttered weakly along the sand, simulating an injured bird. The aim is to lure a predator away from eggs or chicks with the promise of an easy meal. It's a neat trick, but futility itself when deployed against humans with eyes only for each other.

I could see one of the chicks as it moved ahead of the couple, not much bigger than a golf ball, white below, a little darker and softly speckled above – a near-perfect match for the beach. It had a neat trick of its own. I tracked it with binoculars as it whirred along like a clockwork toy, until suddenly it wasn't there any more. Having picked a spot, it had frozen – and vanished – leaving my eyes to roam hopelessly ahead along its predicted path. A predator would now be faced with the difficult task of trying to separate it from its background or, more likely, giving up and seeking food elsewhere. But with four heavy boots approaching, whether it survived or not would be down to luck. I didn't stay to find out.

* * *

Now, to reach the start of the causeway I have a short section of rocky shore to cross. I avoid slippery layers of seaweed as well as the bare, wet surface of the rock itself, and stick to rocks covered with a layer of barnacles, my boots gripping them like Velcro. There's another creature here that builds its own surfaces. On the lowest part of the shore are millions of circular tubes packed tightly together and lying in all directions as they smother the sand and rock. Those that are vertical remind me of organ pipes – Beryl Scott would surely have approved. The surface, where the tubes open to the air, looks like honeycomb, as if the whole thing has been built by great swarms of sea bees. The real architect is the aptly named honeycomb worm. It is just a few centimetres long and works alone, each creature making its own little tube for protection. But before choosing its spot to build, it seeks out company of its own kind; the planktonic larvae sniff out the location of existing tubes and settle close by to begin their work.

In this way, acting alone, in their thousands, then millions, they reshape the shoreline, constructing reefs that trap seawater as the tide leaves. Now there are pools where previously there was bare rock or sand, supporting creatures that would otherwise be forced to retreat with the sea. I feel guilty whenever I inadvertently step on them, though for structures made from sand, they are remarkably resilient, and every bit as slip-resistant as the barnacles. I'm relieved to learn later that they can make good any minor damage at an impressive rate of 4 millimetres of tube per day.[31]

The causeway itself is natural, built up from stones, small rocks and the living mussels that attach to them. In the 1950s, sacks of mussels were collected from around Hestan by fishermen from nearby Kippford. They made a little extra money from a government contract to supply samples to be tested for radioactivity from the new facility at Windscale (now Sellafield) in Cumbria, not far from the mouth of the Solway. Occasionally I've taken a handful of mussels home from the rocks here, though now, a few days into May, it's already a little late in the year. The old rule suggests harvesting shellfish only in months with an 'r' in their name; in the warmer months toxins from bacteria, and especially algae, are more likely to be present.

Across the bay near the hotel at Balcary I can see evidence of resource use of another kind. A ragged, gappy line of wooden poles marches out across the mud from the shoreline. These were once used to support nets, with pockets at the seaward end. At high tide, salmon and other fish would encounter the net and then follow it offshore towards the deeper water, looking for a way around, before ending up trapped in one of the folds of netting.

* * *

By chance, or more likely a shared reading of tides and weather, I've been on the island for no more than half an hour when I bump into Sue Gilroy and her two dogs. She introduces herself and explains that she's here checking up on the sheep. She's braver than I am, having crossed the mud from Balcary, as she does on every visit. 'It's perfectly safe,' she tells me, 'so long as you know the route. I come once a week because

---

31 I learnt this from Ann Lingard's rich and illuminating book about the Solway, which includes more about this extraordinary creature, including the way it reshapes the shoreline and its conservation significance: Lingard, A. (2020) *The Fresh and the Salt: The Story of the Solway*. Birlinn, Edinburgh.

the sheep can get stuck in the brambles, though I cut all the bushes I find. I think I've got most of them.' Perhaps I look surprised, because she pulls out a pair of secateurs and jiggles them back and forth in her palm by way of proof. 'The sheep are on from February to June, for the good spring bite of grass, then we'll come with the dogs and horses and take them back to the hills.' She has a warning for me about overly protective gulls, suggests a good place to look out for otters, and then she's away to complete her circuit of the island before the tide returns. Half an hour later I see her out in the middle of the bay on her way back to shore. There are two more figures heading back to the mainland. I saw them earlier in the garden of the island's old cottage but it seems they were here just for the day. When the tide rises and surrounds the island once more, it looks like I'll be alone.

The 'peak spring' theme is as evident here as it is on the mainland, though Hestan's version is a more raucous affair. There are gull nests everywhere, most already with full clutches. On the gentle grassy slopes in the middle of the island, herring and lesser black-backed gulls are dominant. The gulls' eggs were once collected by local people for sustenance, something that happens now in Britain only at a few colonies on the south coast of England – involving black-headed gulls, the eggs taken under licence for sale into the lucrative restaurant trade.

Herring gulls are also nesting around the fringes of the island on the cliffs, wherever they can find a flat patch of ground, and at the upper end of the small shingle beaches. On the cliffs they are joined by great black-backed gulls. I'd hoped to find this bird here, and based on the number of adults cruising menacingly above the cliffs or sitting on nests there must be at least a dozen pairs. Calling gulls are the default sound of the island. Periodically, they fly up in their hundreds, often for no discernible reason, and the sound rises to a climax before they all settle back down again. Whenever there's a brief, inexplicable lull, it's the sudden absence of noise that feels intrusive; I catch myself looking around, wondering what on earth might have caused it.

From a vantage point near the old lighthouse, I watch a steady stream of cormorants flying shuttles between the rocks and the open sea, some returning with untidy strings of brown seaweed for their nests. I track them back to the rocks, and see that some already have eggs, startlingly white in their dark, weedy setting. Fishing waste has been added to a few nests, including one that has circles of blue weave from an old net. This material can cause real problems for seabirds. The thin, composite strands making up the netting unravel, and if they become wrapped around the legs of chicks, or even adults, the birds may become ensnared, tied firmly into their own nest. When the time comes for them to head out to sea they will watch on, helpless, as their neighbours abandon them to their fate.

On the other side of the island, the usual marine litter has been thrown up to the top of the narrow shingle beaches by winter storms. Strewn among the rocks, some of it is already being incorporated into the ground as the vegetation grows up around it. The waste includes a typical mix of fishing floats, buoys, flip-flops, old fish boxes and tangled masses of rope and nets. The ubiquitous plastic bottles are especially galling. It seems a mild form of insanity to make something designed to be used once from a material that lasts forever. As usual around here, the distinctive yellow and orange bottles of Lucozade are overrepresented compared with the amount of shelf space they take up. Is it the case that seekers of an energy boost are sometimes so lethargic that they are more likely than the average person to carelessly discard their bottle?

I pick up a bottle and carry it a few steps as a spontaneous act of beach cleaning, but amid all this debris the act is futility itself. It still has its lid. In fact, looking around the beach, all the bottles do. It makes sense I suppose. Without a cap a bottle will fill with water and sink, and so is less likely to be washed ashore. But if you're going to launch your empty out of a car window or off the deck of a fishing boat, why bother first replacing the lid? Is this an indication that they've arrived here via a different route? Have they, in fact, been carefully recycled, only to somehow find their way onto our beaches anyway?

The ubiquitous beach sandhoppers have learnt to take advantage of our waste. Lift a clump of seaweed on almost any beach and there's that familiar explosion of life as they throw themselves about, trying to avoid becoming a meal, before slipping away again out of the light. As detritivores they make their living from breaking down organic material. But it has long been known that they will also tackle human artefacts. Naturalist Charles Spence Bate reported back in 1862 that 'a lady's handkerchief which was dropped on a beach for a few minutes was perceived, upon being recovered, to be perforated by myriads of small holes, the work of these creatures … and in their turn these became food for birds, which devoured them greedily.'[32]

It seems the sandhoppers will also tackle more modern materials, including plastics caught up among the seaweed. A single plastic bag can, apparently, be shredded into more than a million tiny pieces.[33] These mini-crustaceans are essentially generators of microplastics on a vast scale, leaving them ready and waiting to be washed out to sea where they are mistaken for tiny creatures and begin their journey up through the food chain. Honed by evolution, marine creatures make the reasonable assumption that anything drifting in the ocean that is small and semi-transparent must be edible. It's an instinct that has served them well for millions of years. But no longer.

There is marine litter of another kind, too. Scattered about the shingle are the tattered bodies of herring gulls, and among them, apparently unperturbed, living birds are hunkered down on their nests. Dead gulls are a recurring theme around the island. In the middle of a national outbreak of bird flu this is a concern. The disease has been responsible for the loss of large numbers of waterbirds in the Solway, with barnacle geese on the major nature reserves of Mersehead and Caerlaverock especially badly affected. Could it have contributed to the deaths of these gulls? I have no way of knowing. On an island with so many live gulls, I have no idea how many bodies would count as abnormally high. But most of the casualties appear long dead, and there are no sluggish or dying birds that would suggest an ongoing outbreak.

Up on the grassy slopes, most of the dead gulls manifest as pointed wing-tips sticking up from holes in the ground. They look like old rabbit holes, and though I've seen no rabbits I've read that they were once here. I'm keen to check the birds for rings, but to do so I have to

---

32 Bate C.S. (1862) *Catalogue of the Specimens of Amphipodous Crustacea in the Collection of the British Museum*. Taylor & Francis, London.
33 Hodgson, D.J., Bréchon, A.L. and Thompson, R.C. (2018) 'Ingestion and fragmentation of plastic carrier bags by the amphipod *Orchestia gammarellus*: Effects of plastic type and fouling load.' *Marine Pollution Bulletin* 127: 154–9.

pull them free. Some are so firmly wedged in place that it takes two hands and no small effort to release them. Sue Gilroy had mentioned that rats were here, and I can only assume that they must be the animal responsible. A dead gull represents a lot of food, but in a place with hordes of living gulls, including the menacing great black-backs, a rat would find it risky to feed out in the open. This would also leave the bodies accessible to other scavengers. So each body is pulled down into the nearest hole. Now the meal can be consumed from below, safe from aerial attack.

After checking dozens of birds, I eventually strike lucky: an adult lesser black-backed gull has a British Trust for Ornithology (BTO) ring. The metal at the edge has been worn away in two places, which I hope means it's an old ring. It's devilishly difficult to remove, but eventually I manage to slide it free over the bird's foot. It would be nice if it has an interesting story to tell. Perhaps the bird was ringed on the island decades ago, returning year after year to rear its young, long before we moved here. Or might it have been ringed as a chick somewhere far away before choosing (as we have done) to settle in this area? Once I get home I will fill in the BTO's online reporting form to find out.

* * *

In the evening, I choose a spot near the top of the cliffs for my sleeping bag. The ground is free of rabbit holes, almost free of sheep droppings, and as close to flat and smooth as I can find. I plan to use the last couple of hours of daylight to look out over the water and the rocky shoreline below me. This is the best way to watch coastal wildlife: find a decent vantage point, sit for long enough so that you start to become part of the scenery, and see what happens by. I pull out my sandwiches, half-expecting to be set upon by a thousand ravenous gulls. But despite the many eyes studying my every move, none of the birds stir. They are in serious breeding season mode, it seems; now is not the time for pilfering scraps.

I scan my telescope across the sea, and one of the first birds that pulls into focus trumps even the rubbish on the beach and the litter of dead gulls as the day's saddest sight. I wish I could unsee it. But once I know it's there, my eyes are repeatedly drawn back. It is floating about a mile offshore, drifting gradually towards the island. I've not seen any wild geese for weeks. They have all headed north to their breeding grounds. Almost all. As the lone pink-footed goose floats ever closer, it becomes obvious why it's here. One wing is hanging down awkwardly, much lower than the other. It might be a victim of wildfowling or perhaps it was injured by flying into overhead wires. Whatever the cause, it hasn't been able to match powerful migratory urges with meaningful action and it has been left behind by its flock-mates. It is, in every sense of the word, adrift.

I need a distraction, and there are plenty about. I can see guillemots and razorbills in the distance, flying out from the cliffs between Balcary and Rascarrel. Nearer the island there's a red-throated diver and dozens of cormorants from the colony, fishing or simply resting on the water. Then, all within a magical 20 minutes, comes a trio of mammals.

I notice 'eyes only' the fleeting black shapes breaking the surface of the grey sea. Zooming in with the telescope I see them resolve, as expected, into harbour porpoises, our smallest cetacean and the only one common in the Solway. They are less than 2 metres long, and surface to breathe with a bare minimum of fuss. A glimpse of the rounded black back with its tiny, triangular dorsal fin is all you can expect to see.

Closer to the rocks is another animal showing only a small part of itself to the terrestrial world. A grey seal head is poking up out of the grey sea. Sometimes they rest (or even sleep) in this position, bobbing along at the surface like bottles. This one is looking around, then it ducks out of sight, only to reappear a few metres away. It is perhaps prospecting for a suitable place on the rocks to haul itself out of the water.

The most complete distraction of all appears almost directly below me. It outscores the porpoises and the seal by showing itself in full as it scampers across the rocks from one watery inlet to another. And it behaves in a way that reveals much more to inquisitive humans about how it lives. I watch as it swims at the surface, investigating all the little nooks and crannies where sea meets rock. It pushes its head into tiny spaces where fish or other creatures might be trying to hide. When it dives it is rarely under water for long, and when successful it has the good grace to bring its food up to the surface so I can see what it's eating. While the unknowability of porpoises and seals lends them a certain magic of their own, sometimes it's nice to be invited further in. I can have a stab at imagining what it might feel like to be an otter, as this one surfaces with a small fish and slides up onto the rocks to feed.

* * *

Before the light goes completely, I walk across to the other side of the island overlooking the bay and the sweep of low hills behind it. From home I look down at Hestan Island every day. It draws the eye, somehow, the way islands do. It feels familiar, so it has been a little surreal spending time here, finally experiencing it first-hand. And now, looking up into the glen, the picture is reversed. This is land I *do* know intimately; it's where I walk every day. And yet from this altered perspective it looks strangely alien and unfamiliar. With the telescope, our house is visible, though I have to hunt to find it, working my way up, farm by farm, from the village below. It is 4 miles away and partially obscured by trees, but I can see the lit window of our bedroom upstairs. Checking the time, I imagine that Hazel is probably there behind it, sitting up in bed reading, an old spaniel snoring alongside. Now that the light has faded, Bengairn and Screel away to the north-east are dark and featureless.

Back on the clifftop, sleep is elusive. I'm kept awake by a combination of relentlessly noisy gulls, the hard surface of the ground and unshakeable thoughts about giant island rats – and then one of the promised rain showers. With no tent, it's a case of pulling the hood of the bivvy bag over my head and lying awake, listening to the soft patter of rain on polyester.

It's light before 5 o'clock, and I need to be up early (though not *this* early) to catch the low tide. I'm still bleary-eyed when I notice the otter again. This time it's well offshore, in fact almost mid-channel between the rocks near Balcary and the island, but getting closer all the time. It is evidently finishing off the mile-long crossing from the mainland. It's a long swim, but the effort involved must be worthwhile. Perhaps the island is too small and too exposed to sustain a resident otter family. But in calm conditions, as today, the rich feeding opportunities will more than make up for the effort of getting here. It reaches the rocks, and I watch it for a while before packing up my things.

The first thing I do when I get home is dig out the gull ring from my rucksack. The initial letter and last two numbers are incomplete because of the missing parts of the ring, but there is enough left to read them. Perhaps I'm guilty of looking for a story, but GN59443 does indeed have one. It was ringed as a nestling in July 2002 on an artificial island in the Wash, off the coast of Norfolk. At the time, Hazel and I were both living in that part of the world, both married to other people, both a year or two away from messy divorces. We worked for English nature in Peterborough, just 25 miles from the Wash, and I visited the site regularly. I saw plenty of lesser black-backs, and – who knows? – perhaps our bird was among them. A lot has happened since then. We've moved around a fair bit and, of course, ended up here in Galloway. No doubt our gull experienced some ups and downs, too, and visited some interesting places. After 21 years, a ripe old age for a lesser black-backed gull, its life ended on a small island within walking distance of our new home.

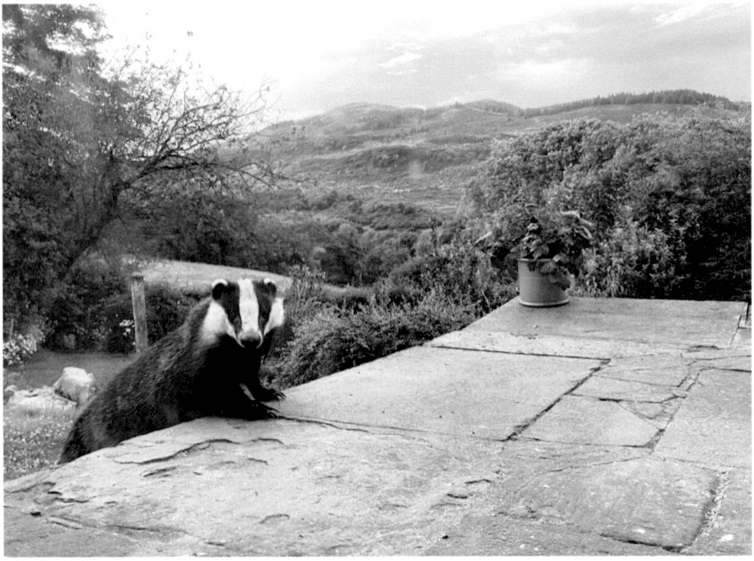

10

House-sharing

Boris, Grandad and hundreds of uninvited summer guests.

Enjoying the benefits of a wildlife garden creates an uneasy counterpoint to a love of the wild places that are free from the obvious day-to-day influence of human activities. In the garden, in contrast, human presence is a constant, our influence is all-pervading, and the relationship between *us* and everything else feels very different.

Still, if you are lucky enough to have a garden you'll probably spend more time watching wildlife in it than anywhere else. It's certainly true for me; our small plot is the only place that I'd claim to know intimately. I'm familiar with every tree, every bush, almost every nesting place. Even now, I find myself looking up, out of the window, distracted by the wildlife that I'm supposed to be writing about. Today, a rather atypical garden bird is getting most of my attention. Less than 100 metres from the house is an old quarry that hosts a small sand martin colony, with just a handful of nest holes. It's so close to home that, delightfully, the birds often join the local swallows to hawk insects above our shrubs and flowerbeds. They sweep elegantly in and out of the airspace, sometimes passing within a metre or two of the windows, before ferrying food back to chicks that have yet to learn there is light in the world. Once the birds leave the garden, their drab plumage makes them difficult to follow against the backdrop of hills. Then, on landing at the entrance to the nest burrows, they vanish completely; they are the colour of the local soil.

I'm confident our garden supports more wildlife than any similar-sized area in the local countryside. Wild animals gravitate towards places with varied, diverse vegetation. And like many gardens, ours has a lot going on in a small space. There are mature trees, including cherry, spruce and several huge, spreading sycamores. There are thick hedges, dominated by beech, hawthorn and evergreen conifers. There are beds full of plants, pathways of open lawn and a pond. Even the buildings help; an old garage and a couple of decaying sheds provide shelter and dry(ish) places to roost and nest. If you are a local song thrush (to take just one example), you'll find tall trees to sing from, dense shrubs to nest in, damp flowerbeds full of snails (and low walls to smash them against), earthworm-rich turf, soft fruit in summer, berries and windfall apples in autumn, and a shallow-fringed pond for bathing. In meeting the needs of wildlife, variety and structural diversity is *everything*.

On the other side of the garden hedge, food-rich places are scarce and they don't last long. Once depleted, it takes a while for them to be replenished – a whole year in the case of berries and nuts. But on our small patio the food is magically renewed each day, as the more astute of the local animals know only too well. An area of no more than 5 by 3 metres sometimes supports more than 50 birds at a time, of perhaps five or six different species, a concentration that would be unthinkable in the nearby woods. They hoover up the food, and then loaf around in the nearby trees, waiting for a human to emerge with more.

Nuthatches, great spotted woodpeckers, and blue, great and coal tits filch peanuts one at a time, consuming them in the cover of a nearby bush. Jays, too, use the grab-and-leave technique, though they have a trick: lots of nuts can be collected at once, packed away into their specially adapted gullet for ease of transport. They are well known, of course, for doing the same thing with acorns. Most ruthlessly efficient of all are the woodpigeons and pheasants. In the time it takes a squirrel to carefully select, manipulate and consume a single nut, holding it delicately between its two front paws, these birds will have complacently swallowed 20 or more.

Chaffinches, goldfinches and house sparrows feed in small flocks, spooking constantly, flying up *en masse* for no obvious reason. But there *is* a reason, and every so often that reason reveals itself. It tries to avoid detection, keeping low to the ground. Then at the last second it flicks up and over the hedge, or flips 90 degrees and flings itself through a narrow vertical gap between hedge and garage. If the initial ambush is unsuccessful, it usually moves on to try its luck elsewhere. Less often, it will hang around and try a different tactic, landing on a bush, or shuffling along the ground beneath, before plunging into the dense foliage. It is seeking out birds that have hidden, and it hopes to get close enough to reach one with its long toes, each of which is furnished with a curved black dagger. If it is successful, the victim will be pinned to the ground, killed (if it's lucky – often, it won't be), plucked and consumed – or carried away to feed a brood of nestlings. Now the relentless neuroticism of the small birds makes sense; better an endless series of false alarms than to risk becoming a sparrowhawk's meal.

* * *

In the artificial, human-dominated space of a garden, the dynamic between observer and the more-than-human world is altered. It's unavoidable, but nonetheless as a lover of wild places I find it unsettling. Rather than observing impassively, as I do elsewhere, constant interventions are the order of the day – interventions that I hope will be beneficial but may not always be so. Here, I am not just watching wildlife; I am meddling with it. That changes the relationship.

We've put up a nestbox, though the blue tits avoid it, preferring a natural hole in the old cherry tree. No matter; they have still become *our* blue tits. I anxiously follow their progress through the season. They work exhaustively hard, as birds must, to raise a family. Every day, hundreds of tiny creatures are ferried back to the nestlings. How do the parents find them all? (Go outside now and try to find even *one* green caterpillar.) By the time the garden fills with fluffy, yellow-faced fledglings, the adults look done for – and yet the begging calls continue; their work is still not complete. All summer long they keep a watchful eye out for the sparrowhawk. And I find myself doing the same thing, hoping they will be spared, pushing the welfare of the sparrowhawk's own nestlings to the back of my mind.

Another example: a plump female toad lived for a while in a damp corner of the garage. One day in late summer there it was, and there it remained through the autumn, always in a slightly different spot. When the weather turned cold it disappeared, presumably having found a place to hibernate. Then, in spring, it – or, by now, was it *she*? – was there again. By late March, toads had begun to join the many palmate newts in the pond, and were busy mating and wrapping their long strings of black eggs around the pondweed, while *she* was still in the garage. I wondered why, and then it dawned on me: she was trapped inside. Rather than creeping in through some unseen cavity as I'd assumed, she must have wandered in through the door we leave open a few inches in summer for the swallows. When it was closed again, once the swallows had headed south, she was stuck. By way of apology, I was tempted to transport her directly to the pond; I think I might even have asked her *out loud* whether she thought that was a good idea. But at this time of year, eager males hang about there, so it's not always the most relaxing of places for a lone female. She would know where it was, I thought, and whether that's where she wanted to go.

Personal pronouns for wild animals are a slippery slope, and we are closer to the bottom with red squirrels and badgers than we are with toads. Certain individuals are easy to recognise by their size, face pattern and fur colour. One of our boldest squirrels has a distinctive, unkempt, bottle-blond tail, and he quickly became known as Boris, after the prime minister of the day. Then there's the old, thick-set boar badger who barges other clan members aside to access his share of the food. He is well meaning enough (we think) but he likes to get his own way. We call him 'Grandad' – but (and I can't stress this enough) not with any particular human role-model in mind.

Unease about an overly personal relationship with wild animals is one thing. But the way we interact with garden wildlife also has real-world impacts. There is increasing evidence that disease spreads more easily when wildlife is concentrated at feeders. This may be true for the squirrel pox virus we fear so much, and the expert advice is to stop feeding if there is a local outbreak. Bird populations too can be seriously affected by diseases that spread more quickly around feeders. Greenfinches have declined dramatically after outbreaks of trichomonosis, and now we see only a handful in the garden. More recently, chaffinch numbers have fallen nationally, with disease again a likely factor, though for now at least, this bird remains common locally.

More indirect effects are also likely. Putting out food benefits the species that are adaptable and flexible enough to make use of it. But whenever one animal gains, others will lose out, most obviously through competition for food or nest sites. Perhaps the redstarts and pied flycatchers that once bred in the woods below the house have gone because they can no longer find places to nest. Perhaps now, come spring, the abundant blue and great tits, eased through the winter with abundant food, have already taken all the best sites.

These are tricky issues. We grumble about the intensification of farming and the haemorrhaging of wildlife from the countryside, but in our own gardens we alone are in control; it is the one place where we can make a real difference, and that is no small thing.

*　*　*

We live more intimately with one creature than any other, although we don't do anything to encourage it. It is not interested in handouts. But it connects our home to the wider landscape more effectively than any other animal, arriving in its hundreds during the early summer and staying for a few months while the next generation of young is reared. It scatters mouse-like droppings around the outside of the house, peppering the windowsills and the glass roof of the conservatory. And every evening, as the light starts to fade, we look out for it. Small bodies climb up inside the cavity walls, chittering gently to each other – or to themselves – before spilling out into the air. Others appear as if by magic at the apex of the roof, having emerged from unknowable nooks and crannies beneath the tiles. They fly down to the sheltered, wooded glen below to begin the night's foraging. Watching from the garden on a still, warm evening, we are reminded by the local midges that there is no shortage of food.

This far north the summer nights are short and the transition from light to dark is delightfully slow. Often the earliest, presumably hungriest, bats are in the air before the last of the swallows have given it up for the day. For a short time each day, flying insects have multiple problems to contend with. The bats would prefer total darkness of course. They hunt by echolocation. Light doesn't help them find food, but it does mean they have more chance of *becoming* food. The swallows are old hands at this game and are presumably better adapted to deal with the threat; like all small birds, they must be ready for it all day, every day. When a sparrowhawk appears in the garden, they rise up in a swirling mass, alarm-calling frantically, to show that they have spotted it, and to encourage it on its way: *You've been noticed. You'll have no luck with your ambush attacks here, so you may as well clear off and try someplace else.*

It doesn't always work. On an early July afternoon I watched dumbfounded as a peregrine managed to outfox them. It flew towards the house at height from the nearby hills. When directly above the garden it turned and stooped towards the ground at such speed that I couldn't follow it with binoculars. So I was watching 'eyes only' as it smashed hard into one of the hirundines milling around above the garden, decelerating sharply to pull out of its dive. It was too late now, but defensive reflexes kicked in and the swallows (and a few house martins), now one fewer in number, mobbed and chided the raptor as it headed back to the hills. No doubt the mobbing birds included siblings, parents or perhaps even the partner of the corpse now held firmly in the peregrine's talons.

The bats are wary, too. Often, they leave the roost in small groups, three or four departing in quick succession. I suspect that whenever one leaves it persuades a few other waverers to take the plunge. So there are gaps when the sky is empty, interspersed with little flurries of activity. This makes sense. If a predator should be passing, there is added security in not being the only potential meal available. The bats head out with real purpose, flying fast and straight, keen to reach their feeding grounds and the shelter of the trees below as quickly as possible. Those that skim low over our heads while we watch register as an audible whir as they shoot out into the evening.

I was surprised to learn that when foraging our bats roam further afield than the dayshift of hirundines. Swallows find most of their food within a few hundred metres of their breeding site. Those with nests in our outbuildings use the fields immediately surrounding the house. In contrast, studies of pipistrelles have shown that they will travel up to a few kilometres from their roost, seeking out the places richest in flying insects, and taking up to 3,000 in a single night by scooping them up in the membrane of their tails, and then, while still in flight, bending down to eat good mouthfuls of them.

By sitting outside in the evening we've found that most of the bats leave within a window of around half an hour. I've taken to counting them in this peak, 30-minute, period at dusk. The current record is 192 and numbers tend to rise towards the end of summer, when the young of the year are old enough to venture outside, swelling the ranks. If they all feed well, then by the time the sun creeps up again in the eastern sky there might be *half a million* fewer flying insects.

When the bats return in the early morning the chittering begins again. We can hear it inside the walls by our bed. They scrabble and squabble just a few inches away from our heads, perhaps jostling for the best positions from which to see out the long hours of daylight. We're used to it now, which is just as well, as in midsummer it can start up not long after 3 am. Much like bird song through an open window, it is soothing to me rather than irritating. They have made it back home once again after a night out, and I'm glad of their company for a while as I drift off back to sleep. As in the evening, they sometimes overlap with the swallows, which may already be up and about as the last of the bats settle into their roost.

Watching from the garden as the bats arrive back shows them in a new light, though it requires a *very* early start. I stumbled into the spectacle by accident. Our elderly spaniel had woken me up, needing to go outside. Knowing I wouldn't get back to sleep I made a coffee and took it out into the garden. And there they were, swarming about the apex of the roof just above me; a massed, swirling, high-energy vortex of bats, involving at least a dozen individuals. Every few seconds, one would break ranks and slip away into the roost, to be replaced in the swarm by new animals arriving back from the foraging grounds.

Using Hazel's bat detector we learnt that our bats were a mixture of common and soprano pipistrelles. Things were simpler once; the small bats I watched in childhood (and tossed pebbles to, so they would dive down, thinking they might be moths) were all simply 'pipistrelles'. Then in the 1980s ecologists realised that there were in fact two closely related species, best distinguished by their vocalisations. As you might have guessed, the soprano has the higher-pitched call. They can also be separated by subtle differences in appearance, though examination in the hand is needed for that. We wondered if we might one day find a dead bat. But we went one better: we caught a live one.

Watching the evening news, we had already noticed a few early-emergers flying out over the garden when we became aware of a strange scrabbling noise. Off went the TV. There it was again, clearer now. Hazel's ears are sharper than mine, and she quickly traced the sound to an open-topped circular lampshade covering one of the wall lights in the room. Near the top there is a small gap between the light bulb and the surrounding glass of the shade. The hapless creature had managed to slip through it to the base below. It must have entered the room through an open window the night before. Unable to work out how to get back outside, it had found a secure place to see out the day. Now it was keen to leave, but the smooth surface of the glass was impossible to climb. And with the gap between the bulb and the shade so narrow, it couldn't unfurl its wings fully in order to fly out. It had stumbled upon an object that might as well have been purpose-built as a bat trap. We offered it the sleeve of a jumper which it duly climbed. And before it flew from Hazel's palm as she stood by the open door, I took a photo. It shows the dark, bandit-mask across the face that reveals this individual to be a common pipistrelle.

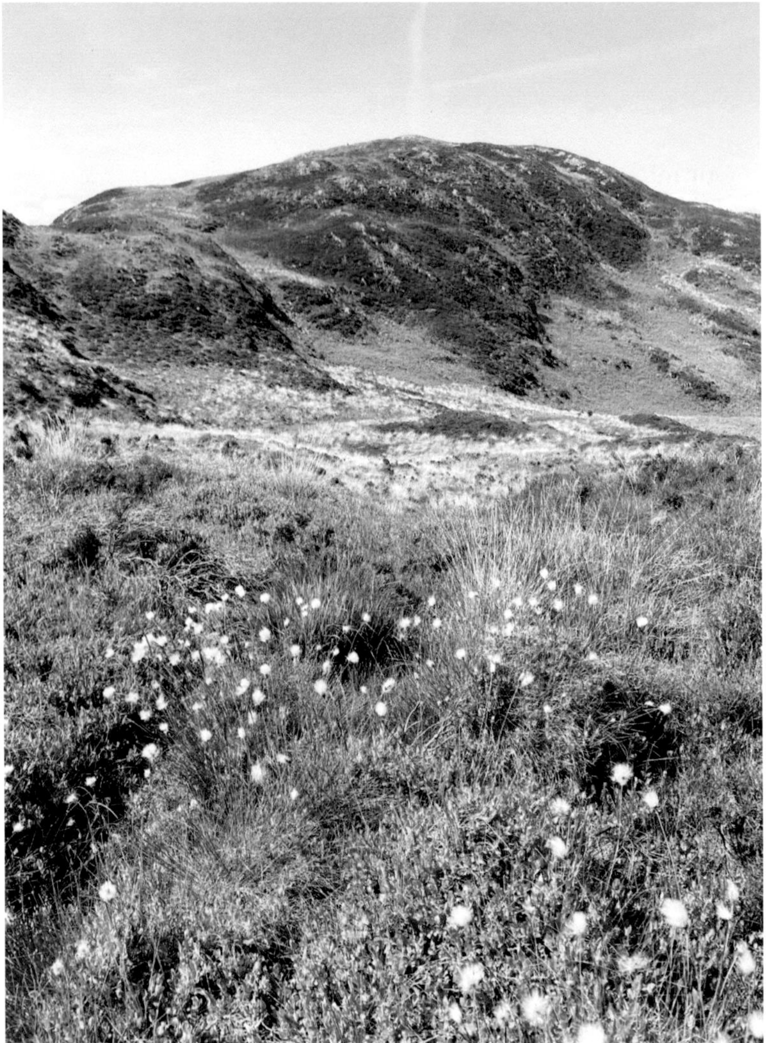

11

The high tops

Our mini-mountain, its grouchy resident, and the ancient human yearning to get to the top.

The stature of a hill is influenced by its height, obviously enough, but also by the way it fits into the landscape. The stone cairn and trig point on Bengairn are nearly 400 metres above sea level. (Screel Hill, about a mile away, is a little lower.) For perspective, the distinctive round dome of Criffel, which dominates the skyline as you venture west into Galloway, is 569 metres, and Ben Nevis, Britain's highest mountain, away to the north, is 1,345 metres. *Our* high tops, then, are big hills rather than anything grander. But because the land drops away rapidly in all directions, they stand out. From below, especially if you are contemplating the climb, Bengairn feels like a mountain. When it has a dusting of snow, or when cloud is swirling around the top on an otherwise calm and sunny day, it is more imposing still.

The wide southern flank of Bengairn dominates the view from our garden. I can just about make out the cairn at the top without binoculars, and with no dawdling can be standing on top of it, looking back down to the house, in about 90 minutes. There is no path and accordingly, almost always, no people. The walking is hard, though. There are burns to cross, old stone dykes to clamber over, plantations to avoid, and patches of thick heather and bracken to battle through. In early summer, new bracken shoots push up through the tangled thatch of last year's dead plants. The old, dry stems crunch underfoot, shattering into spiky shards. Inevitably, they find their way into your boots where they bite at the flesh until you are forced to pause for a while to remove them.

Away from the bracken, boggy areas are lit in summer with drifts of fluffy white cottongrass. They can be hazardous places to walk. Unless you come in wellies – and even then are willing to get wet – you'll need to pick the right conditions. A long dry spell helps, though the bogs hold so much water they never fully dry out. In winter, a few days of sub-zero temperatures makes all the difference; low mounds of sphagnum moss stiffen with ice, and surface pools solidify. Now you might find a way across the surface, supported by the land rather than sinking down into it.

We are so used to walking on paths that straying from them can take a bit of relearning. It's a case of trying to relax about not having a fixed line to follow; choosing a route based on things seen and the way the terrain opens up ahead; and treating the bracken shards and the waterlogged ground for what they are – minor and temporary inconveniences rather than serious obstacles to progress. Then, the experience is enriched; with responsibility for finding your own way comes a subtly enhanced connection to the land – all of the land, in its many guises, not just a thin, pre-determined line.[34]

Once I've climbed the final stone dyke, it's just open, rocky moorland between me and the summit. A few sheep graze up here. The densities are low, but grazing, together with the cooler, more exposed conditions, helps keep the vegetation in check. The heather is shorter now and the walking easier. Bushes and young trees are scattered thinly about the moorland. The hawthorns will have been planted by birds, and probably by mammals too. They feast on berries, and deposit the seeds, ready fertilised, wherever they happen to roam next. Sitka spruce seeds drift in on the wind from the forests below. Most conservationists would wish them gone. But they add variety and structure, and as they are self-sown, they are dotted randomly across the moor. They are not natural, but at least they *look* natural. This whole area would once have been cloaked in forest. What, then, is worse: no trees or trees of the wrong kind?

---

34 Screel Hill is an easier walk than Bengairn. It's closer to the road. There are tracks leading through plantations on the lower slopes and a waymarked path (albeit a little rough and ready) up to the summit. The view from the top is every bit as impressive. You probably won't have the place to yourself, especially in summer, but if you prefer to avoid the bogs and bracken and want to be able to follow a well-defined route, this is the best hill to choose.

Outcrops of bare rock add variety to the slopes, and the flatter sections make good places to walk; a welcome escape, for a few metres, from the bogs, the bracken and the wiry, grasping stems of heather. The rock surface is a muted grey-green with a few patches of pink. It looks as if a pink lichen has started to colonise. But it's the other way around. The granite here has a natural pinkish tinge which has been erased for the most part by the soft, pastel shades of the lichens.

Whichever route I take, I always spend a few minutes at the top. From there, the landscape stretches out in all directions.[35] Inland are the high hills of Galloway Forest Park, rolling away into the distance – a national park in waiting if recent pronouncements by the Scottish government are anything to go by. To the south, the peaks of the Lake District rise up on the far side of the Solway – higher hills still, with national park status already safely secured. And over the Irish Sea, to the south-west, the distinctive low, bumpy outline of the Isle of Man. That's not a good sign, according to our local weather lore: 'if you can see the Isle of Man, it's going to rain; if you *can't* see it, it's already raining'. It's not true, though: there are times when light rain is falling and yet the unmistakable outline is still faintly discernible through the murk.

Only one thing snags the eye. Or rather an assemblage of 58 things. The wind farm of Robin Rigg out in the Solway. We need clean power, so it's churlish to grumble; but the turbines are intrusive in a way that few other structures can match. They seem designed to be so. They're colossal, gleaming white in the sun, with vast blades that carve through the air – and through seabirds that are off with their timing. Look in any other direction and there is reassuring evidence that not everything is about humanity. There is human infrastructure, of course; distant roads, farms, villages and even small towns are folded into the hills. Humans are present here, yes, but as just one part of a diverse, half-wild landscape. The turbines, however, strike a different pose. From 12 miles away they scream of dominance and control. That we need

---

35 The East Stewartry Coast National Scenic Area (broadly, NSAs are the Scottish equivalent of England's AONBs) covers an expanse of local hill country and coastline, running away to the north-east. It includes the tops of Bengairn and Screel – but rather surprisingly the western boundary tracks the flanks of Bengairn so that most of our glen is excluded. I'm biased, of course, but that feels like a bit of an oversight.

something so vast speaks of the scale of the problems we face – and, we are told, *still* they are not enough.

* * *

I come to Bengairn for the space, the quiet and (wind farm excepted) the views. I also come for the birds, though near the top there tend to be rather few; a handful of skylarks, the ubiquitous meadow pipits and a pair or two of stonechats breed on the higher slopes. A raven might fly over, letting you know it's coming with a resounding 'gronk', and gulls and woodpigeons drift silently across, on their way to somewhere else. Swifts make it up here too, sometimes. They seek out concentrations of flying insects, wherever that takes them, straying tens of miles from their nests if they need to. When conditions are right, they grace the skies above Bengairn, appearing insignificant against the scale of the landscape but significant beyond measure in what they stand for. I rarely see them without thinking of Ted Hughes' famous poem: 'Look! They're back! Look! … They've made it again … the globe's still working'. In the moment, watching as they scythe wide arcs back and forth above the moors, I really believe it's true.

There is another bird here. It signifies little about the way the globe works, but its presence is reassuring nonetheless when it comes to this small corner of our planet. It is tough, able to live year-round on the high ground while other birds drop to lower levels at the first hint of winter. It subsists largely on heather. On moors managed for shooting, patches of vegetation are burnt in rotation to provide a reliable supply of nutritious new growth, predators are swept away, and medicated grit is provided in plastic trays scattered across the moor, to reduce outbreaks of disease. But Bengairn's red grouse inhabit a wilder landscape. Thick heather offers shelter and places where a nest might be hidden. Close-cropped vegetation around the rocky outcrops, and where sheep have been grazing, provides new shoots. And the wet areas, hazed with cottongrass, are where the females will lead their chicks to feed on invertebrates.

These hills are an isolated outpost for grouse. On some of my visits all I find are a few piles of the distinctive, fibrous droppings. It's good to know the birds are still here, even if the evidence is second-hand. But it's not the same as seeing the creature itself. The trick, I've found, is to forget about them. Only then might a pair or two spring up from thick cover before flinging themselves away across the hill, skimming low over the moor, coughing and spluttering disapproval as they go. Their speed and agility is impressive, and that's what makes it such a desirable sporting bird. Even tucked away in a grouse butt, with birds pushed directly overhead by flag-waving beaters, hitting one as it hurtles by towards safety is a challenge.

The grouse supplement their diet in high summer, once the bilberries begin to ripen; it's a welcome change, no doubt, from the relentless munching of dry heather shoots. Back in Devon, this plant was less common and the competition for berries intense. Finding a bush bearing ripe berries was a rare event and, if you picked them, a guilty pleasure; you were depriving the local wildlife of food. Here, they are abundant and the birds and mammals simply can't keep up.

Every year, then, in mid-July, I return to these high slopes, being careful to choose a day with sufficient breeze to hold the midges at bay. (On a calm day *walking* is one thing; it's bearable – the midges struggle to keep up. But pausing to gather berries hands them the advantage.) I come home with purple-stained lips and fingers, and a full ice-cream tub for the freezer. The garden's blackcurrant bushes produce a glut of fruit, enough to see us through the winter. But the bilberries offer something else: a taste of high summer in the high hills.

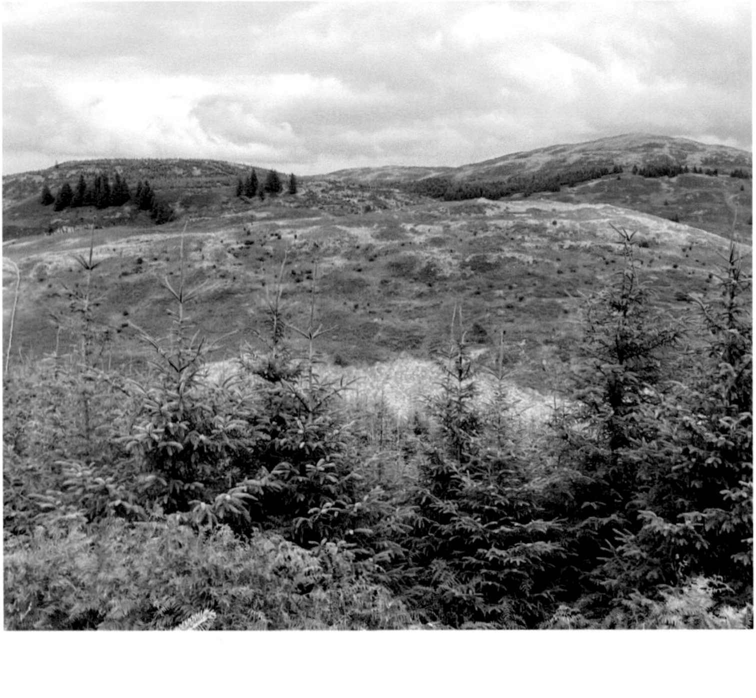

12

The eagle's way

Looking out for a special bird, and what it means when I see it.

'Are there eagles where you live now?' we're asked, with a mixture of curiosity and envy, when friends hear that we've moved to southern Scotland. It's a simple enough question. But I find myself pausing and gathering my thoughts before explaining that the answer is, well, a little complicated.

Our glen and the surrounding hills were once prime eagle country. Thanks to reduced persecution and the efforts of conservationists, it seems likely they will become so once again. But for now we are in a kind of limbo; an indefinable state somewhere between eagle country and normal countryside. Mostly, when it comes to large raptors, we make do with the abundant buzzards (the 'tourist eagle'), red kites, and the less frequent goshawks. But every so often a larger bird appears. It causes a stir among the locals – human and avian. When I mention that I've seen one, our neighbours start to look out for it. And a good way to find it is to keep an eye on the resident buzzards and corvids. When they whip themselves into a frenzy and start to dive down at a bird that seems in comparison almost too big to be real, then your luck is in.

As yet, golden eagles do not breed in our corner of Galloway. Come the summer, there will be no hungry young waiting in a vast stick nest to be fed. We must content ourselves with irregular and unpredictable visits from lone, wandering birds. Months slip by without a sighting. Then one day I'll raise my binoculars to a distant raptor to check whether it's a buzzard or a red kite – and gasp as it resolves into neither. The day is made. And as I walk on, I'll spare a thought for the local brown hares and the handful of red grouse that cling on in the hills. Now they will have to up their game.

Jim Crumley suggested in his book *The Eagle's Way* that 'this eagle is nature's ambassador, the catalyst that stirs wildness into its most primitive endeavours.'[36] It's true. On days when I see an eagle, the place feels different. It feels *wilder*. When I don't see one – and after all that is most days – there is something missing, something more than the absence of the bird itself. Human ambassadors paint the country they represent in the best possible light. Without nature's ambassador our glen feels not quite whole. And my mind drifts more easily from the wildlife that remains here to all that has been lost.

The golden eagle and the even larger white-tailed eagle (or sea eagle, as I prefer to call it) have both suffered at our hands. Long before poisons and firearms made things easier, we found ingenious ways to kill them. One was as simple as a narrow trench baited with a dead animal. Once the bird had dropped inside, it would have no room to unfurl its huge wings to effect a rapid escape. It could be ambushed by the hunter rushing towards it, or caught in a noose placed at the end of the trench as it tried to walk to safety. Another method involved waiting concealed within a roofed pit dug into the ground, with only a narrow slit remaining open. Bait was placed close to the opening and, no doubt with considerable patience, when an eagle landed it could be caught by thrusting a long arm through the slit and grabbing its legs. It works; the technique has survived into modern times in Norway, where conservationists have used it to catch eagles for ringing.

The sea eagle is less wary of humans than the golden eagle, and so it was (and still is) an easier bird to kill. Golden eagles were certainly impacted by persecution; their numbers fell and they were lost from many places, Galloway included. But for the sea eagle matters were altogether more serious. Once, it easily outnumbered the golden eagle. And yet by 1918 there was just a single bird remaining: an old, pale individual in Shetland. It too was shot, despite protestations from local people. Amazingly, a grainy, dimly lit photograph of this bird exists, showing it resting on a cliff ledge, its pale plumage glowing out eerily

---

36 Crumley, J. (2014) *The Eagle's Way: Nature's New Frontier in a Northern Landscape.* Saraband, Glasgow.

from a backdrop of dark rock. It is reproduced in John Love's book *A Saga of Sea Eagles*, the author noting that it is 'undoubtedly the only photograph ever taken of a truly British Sea Eagle, the last of its race indeed.'[37]

* * *

Sea eagles are making a comeback thanks to a pioneering reintroduction programme that started in 1975, when the first young birds were flown in from Norway. There are now around 150 pairs in Scotland, and although it has yet to return to Galloway to breed, young birds visit occasionally, attracted especially to the long, prey-rich shoreline of the Solway. We live just 2 miles from the north shore, and I often pause to watch from a window if I notice the wintering pink-footed and barnacle geese lifting from the coastal fields, spooked by something unseen. They chatter to themselves as they decide where best to resettle. And I search the sky to see if I can find the source of the disturbance. One day soon, I hope, it will be a sea eagle drifting along the shoreline, looking for signs of weakness in the flock below and the chance of a meal.

For now though, we make do with our golden eagles. Elsewhere in Galloway they have a tenuous foothold as breeding birds with a handful of pairs, and the small population in southern Scotland has been given a boost through the release of both young and older birds taken from healthy populations further north. Southern Scotland now supports around 50 birds and it is hoped that numbers will continue to increase.

Hazel and I saw our first golden eagle in early April, just six weeks after we'd moved in. We watched transfixed from the garden as it drifted along the ridge that runs up to the top of Bengairn. Two red kites nearby provided scale, no longer the largest things in the air and buffeted by the wind even as the heavier, more powerful bird held steady on its course. It landed on the cairn of stones at the summit. By chance, only a few days earlier I'd been sitting on that cairn with my two grown-up children, looking back at the house. Now the telescope was pointing in the opposite direction and a golden eagle was contemplating its next

---

[37] Love, J.A. (2013) *A Saga of Sea Eagles*. Whittles Publishing, Dunbeath.

move on the exact spot where we'd eaten our lunch. I could just make out the thin wire of a satellite tag sticking up from the bird's back. I got in touch with Cat Barlow, manager of the South of Scotland Golden Eagle Project, to let her know where her bird was (of course, she knew already), and I learnt that it was a young male, fledged from a nest in Galloway in the previous summer. For now, he wanders the hills of southern Scotland, and will hopefully continue to do so for several years before he is old enough to pair up and settle down to breed.

I can't help but find these tags ugly. As adornments added by human hands, they sap a little of the bird's majesty and wildness – but they do provide invaluable information about how eagles move through the landscape. And they add a layer of protection. There are still people who wish these birds gone, worrying that they will deplete stocks of gamebirds or predate livestock. Society is becoming less tolerant of these attitudes and at the same time the technology is making it ever more difficult for people to take the law into their own hands and get away with it.

In mid-December another young golden eagle appeared, this time without a tag. It stayed for several weeks, gracing the glen for the darkest and, as it turned out, coldest weeks of the year. We saw it most days in the lead-up to Christmas, sometimes close enough to make out the bird's crop, swollen with food, as it passed overhead. It must have found a reliable source of meat, perhaps a sheep or deer carcass, or the gralloch[38] from a deer killed by one of the local stalkers – enough to keep it here, for a while at least. It moved on, as we knew it would. But it, or others of its kind, will be back. Slowly but surely we are becoming part of the eagle's way once more.

* * *

There is another large raptor in the area. It's not an eagle, but its impressive size and spectacular behaviour lend it the much the same

---

[38] 'Gralloch' refers both to the innards of a deer and the process of removing them. This is often done in the field to help maintain the quality of the meat (and make the carcass a little easier to carry) and can be a valuable source of food for scavengers. The word is derived from the Gaelic for 'intestines' and has become the commonly used term among deer stalkers.

stature. Old Scottish names suggest that birdwatchers of the past agreed: it was once known as the eagle fisher or water eagle. The osprey shares the white-tailed eagle's history of decline and loss; its predilection for fresh fish would not have gone unnoticed, as well as making it an easy bird to find and kill. By 1916 it had been harried to extinction in Britain.

Fortunately, its migratory habit gave it a lifeline. Whereas the eagle was unlikely to find its way back to Scotland unaided, ospreys on the long return journey from West Africa to Europe continued to visit us. Mostly they were lone strays blown off course, or birds hurrying through en route to Scandinavia. But eventually a few decided to stay. There is debate about when exactly they returned, but by the mid-1950s there was no doubt; the long story of their comeback had begun. It is far from finished, but now there are over 250 pairs in Scotland, and through a combination of natural spread and reintroductions they are slowly returning to England and Wales too.

The National Trust for Scotland's Threave Estate, just down the road, hosts a well-known and much-loved pair of ospreys. We visit sometimes, to catch up with them (and to impress our visitors), and to take in the peregrines that nest on Threave Island's ancient, crumbling castle. The opportunity to see both nesting peregrines and ospreys on the same river island, both easily viewable from the footpath, is surely unique in Britain. (There is also a red kite feeding station at Bellymack Farm, a few minutes' drive away from Threave; raptor afficionados are certainly well catered for in this corner of Galloway.)

At first, it felt greedy to hope to see ospreys close to home, but there were grounds for optimism. The staff at Threave had mentioned to us that their birds wander up to 10 miles from the nest to visit reliable fishing spots. As it happens, we are 7 miles away, and the Solway another 3 beyond that – so 10 miles exactly. Based on watching the fish-eating birds and fish-catching humans, it's clear to me that the bay near Auchencairn has plenty of food. And sure enough, in mid-April of our second year, alerted by irate herring gulls, I watched an osprey flying close to the cliffs at Balcary, flapping vigorously over the water towards land. A few days later there was another (or – who knows? – perhaps the same bird), this time flying through the heart of the glen.

It was plying its way steadily north-west, its long, narrow wings arched and gull-like, in typical osprey fashion. Very likely it was returning to Threave. As it disappeared into the low hills it probably wouldn't see another human for the next few miles. But back at the nest there would be a steady stream of admiring visitors to the watch point, to welcome it home.

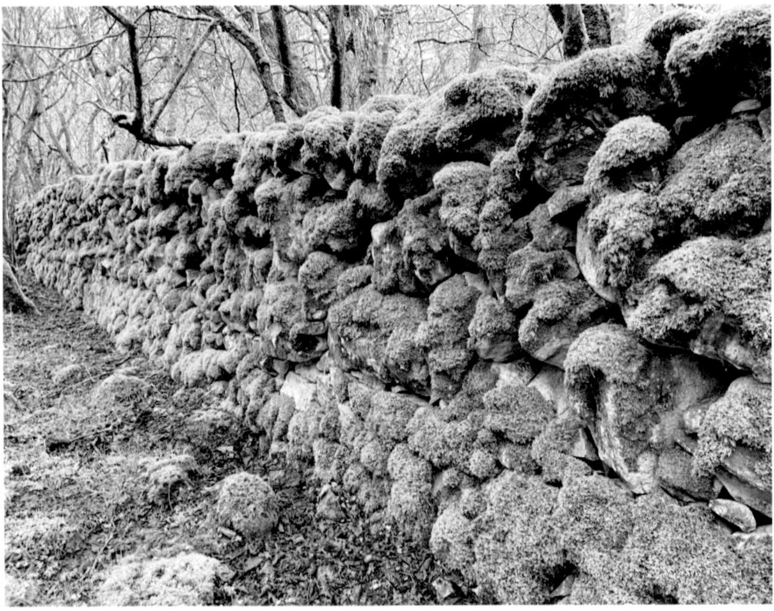

13

A million stones

Dykes, smoots and jooks, and the animals that use them.

Dry-stone dykes, centuries old, run uninterrupted for mile upon mile through the local countryside. They criss-cross the rough pastures, where they help to keep livestock on one side or the other. And they run up into the afforested hill country beyond. They add character and beauty to the landscape, and they provide resting and sheltering places for wildlife.

In the hills, the dykes are redundant, the livestock long gone. They show up on an Ordnance Survey map I have dating back to 1893, running the same lines across the terrain long before the trees appeared. Who knows when they were first built? But here they remain, looking increasingly incongruous as alien conifers spring up all around them. They do at least provide walkable lines through the landscape: narrow corridors open to the sky, where light floods down to the ground. Heather, bracken and bilberry grow well here, offering a reminder of the ancient hill country, deep within the new forests.

In the deciduous woods lower down, bank voles and wood mice make use of myriad cracks and crevices between the stones to hide their stores of hazelnuts. The nuts with neat round holes in the shell have already been consumed. The dykes serve as a useful refuge, though care is needed; predators use them too. For buzzards and the night-shift of tawny and barn owls they make handy lookout points, especially in treeless areas where perches are otherwise in short supply. Regurgitated pellets show where the raptors have rested a while to digest a meal – the bones and fur of the unfortunate rodents returned to the dyke one final time.

In summer, dykes on south-facing slopes soak up the sun's heat, and the stones hold onto it. They become good places to find animals that crave warmth. The aptly named wall brown butterfly has two long-lasting generations each summer, so can be seen throughout the warmer months of the year. It is in the same family as the more common, and far drabber, meadow brown. When one basks on a stone, the full beauty of its wings is revealed – a fritillary-like checkerboard of gleaming orange panels and black, white-dotted eyespots. They use the dyke itself, but mostly I notice them on individual stones that have slipped down to the turf below. Sun-bathed stones are also good places to look for common lizards. As cold-blooded reptiles, a little extra heat from the sun is just what they need to warm up and become active. In the cool Galloway summer, a few degrees can make all the difference.

One potential downside for wildlife is the way that dykes restrict movements: they make effective barriers for wild, as well as domestic, animals. Humans, at least, are well catered for. Whoever first built them thoughtfully incorporated flat, protruding stones in a series of steps, at regular intervals. I find them invaluable, but mostly they see little use these days. The growth of mosses and lichens on these steps is little disturbed by human feet.

Wild mammals have their own ways of getting across. For the agile red squirrel and pine marten, the dykes are no obstacle. In fact, they provide useful lines of transit, the tops being far easier to negotiate than the thick hill-country vegetation of heather and bracken, and they offer a good view of the surroundings. For most other creatures it's a case of finding a way *through*. Wood mice and other small mammals can slip easily between the stones. Badgers must find another way, but they are obdurate and persistent, seeking out points of weakness in the base and using powerful claws to pull loose stones out of the way. In doing so they help other creatures. These runs see a regular passage of animals, evidenced by the worn paths of vegetation on either side of the hole. My camera trap catches foxes and brown hares at these crossing points, as well as badgers. All three animals commute regularly between the pastures of the farm and the hill country above, slipping quietly through the dykes that divide them.

Roe deer have a different approach. For them, *over* is the best option, though they prefer to find places where some of the upper stones have fallen so that the leap becomes easier.

The humble mole might have the neatest method of all. Sometimes I find molehills on both sides of a dyke. The piles of soil are there in the field, but extend into the woods or the edge of the hill country on the far side. It's possible they involve different individuals – but I suspect that moles do what comes naturally, and tunnel their way *under* in order to get from one side to the other. In late winter, the far side of the farm dyke is the safest place to be. That's when the mole-catcher does his rounds, black labrador perched precariously on top of the quad bike next to a box full of shiny metal traps.

Some of our local dykes have purpose-built holes, carefully incorporated into the base when they were first constructed. The ones I've found are small – but, as I quickly learnt from social media, larger ones, known as lunkies or creep holes, were built to enable sheep to pass through. They could be closed off with a large stone when necessary. The smaller holes I've seen would not do for sheep, but they are large enough for hares, foxes and badgers. They go by a variety of local names in different parts of the country, including smoot/smout holes and jook or jouk holes.

Would they have been installed to help wildlife move unimpeded through the landscape, or to reduce the risk of the dyke being damaged by a determined badger? Perhaps. Although there is a darker, and I think more likely, interpretation, in keeping with the prevailing attitudes of the day: these gaps, where mammals pass predictably from one side to the other, would have made ideal places to leave a trap or snare.

I sometimes disturb a fox during the day in one of the pasture fields. If there's woodland nearby, that's where it will run to seek refuge. But on the higher slopes it will make off towards the cover of the forestry land on the far side of the boundary dyke, running in a straight line to the nearest smoot hole. These animals know their patch intimately; they know where all the gaps are.

If left alone for long enough, the dykes face the same fate as anything built by humans: first they are colonised by nature, then they are slowly pulled apart. In the bottom of the glen and along burns, the dykes become furred with a thick layer of moss. It spreads over the stones, softening their edges, turning each one into a plush green cushion before filling the gaps between them. Other plants use the moss to gain traction; ferns and even tree seedlings begin to emerge, and bramble and ivy scrambles over the surface, providing cover for birds, and berries for pigeons and thrushes.

Higher up in the hills, where the terrain is more exposed, the stones are covered with lichen instead of moss. I'm not good with lichens, but the distinctive map lichen is one I've come to know. As it grows, this partnership of algae and fungi forms irregular patches dominated by the algal partner but with the fungus visible as a thin black line marking the boundary between one patch and the next. Contrived countries build into continents, painting the rock in pastel shades of green and yellow.

Map lichen can be used to age buildings and rock-falls by finding the largest specimens and using known growth rates to estimate how long they would have taken to reach that size. Some, in the Arctic, are thought to have been growing for thousands of years, making them among the oldest organisms on our planet.[39] A study in North Wales (the closest to Galloway that I could find) produced one of the higher growth rates: around 1.5 millimetres a year. The largest of the lichen countries here in our glen reach up to 8 centimetres across. They don't look much, these thin slithers of life on the ancient stones. But they have been alive, some of them, for as long as I have.

Lichens are easy to overlook or take for granted, but they supposedly cover more of the Earth's surface than rainforests, and are a force of nature to be reckoned with. They make a living by extracting nutrients from the rock. And eventually they will help turn the old dykes here into soil.

Humans help with the slow process of decay. In the hills, sections of dyke have been dismantled by foresters wanting to be able to step easily from one side to the other. On the farmland below, when holes appear the dyke is sometimes repaired. But it's a slow and skilful process; if time is short, a quick and easy solution is always available – wooden

---

[39] Sheldrake, M. (2020) *Entangled Life: How Fungi Make Our Worlds, Change Our Minds, and Shape Our Futures.* Vintage, Dublin.

pallets or rolls of wire mesh fencing are used to plug the gaps. Dyke-making is a dwindling art, yet what has persisted up to now has been built to last; Galloway's stone dykes will outlive those of us who walk these landscapes, pausing every so often to admire them.

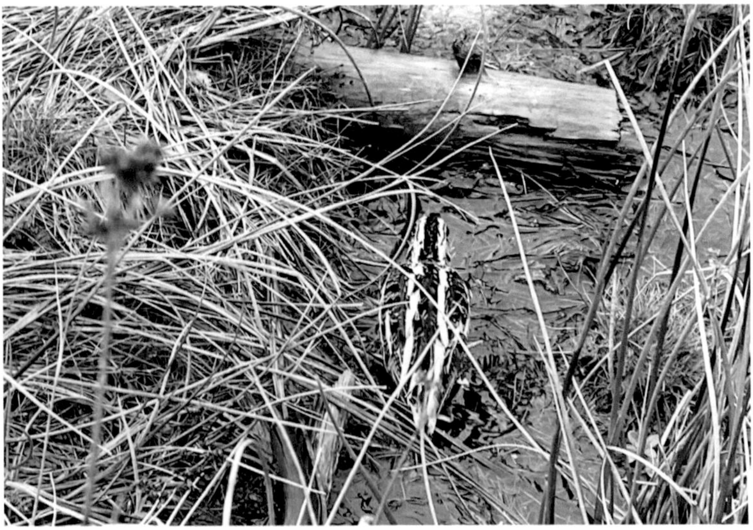

14

A watering hole in the hills

A trio of winter waders, and gatherings of dragons in the late-summer lull.

On the lower slopes of Bengairn there's an isolated pond. It's oval with a large, well-vegetated island, where a lone pair of Canada geese sometimes nest, surrounded by a doughnut of shallow water from which a mallard or two – or on a good day a pair of teal – might fly up. It sits just below an old forest track, and must have been dug with heavy machinery, either as a conservation measure or to provide water in case of fire – or perhaps a bit of both. To reach it from the house, I have two options. I can either walk up the farm track and then follow a long loop of forest road: a five-mile round trip, but the walking is easy. Or I can take the short cut, a straight line of about half a mile, which involves hopping the stone dyke between farm and hill country, and then scrambling up the slope on the far side.

This slope was cleared of its conifers a few years ago, although the next crop is already in the ground. As well as the rocky outcrops, there are old conifer stumps and long piles of brash left over from the previous crop of trees. The resurgent vegetation includes dense, unbalancing tussocks of grass, and spiky arches of brambles that snag and tug at the legs. Walking through it is a battle. So when I come here to the pond, it's usually because I'm looking for something special that will make the effort worthwhile.

In winter, it's the waterlogged margins that provide the magic. This is the only place locally where I can reliably find snipe, together with their rarer and less skittish cousin, the jack snipe. There are subtle differences in size and structure between these birds, but it's the wiring of their nervous systems that sets them apart. The snipe is on perpetual high alert. Its eyes are set wide apart on the side of its head, making it impossible to approach one unseen from any direction. Like the rabbit and hare, this is not a creature that ever faces *away* from anything. As soon as a human shape is registered off it goes, rising up from the ground, firing off its muffled sneezes and hurtling away into the distance, zig-zagging frantically, as if trying to dodge a bullet. As a bird that can legally be shot, it knows what it's doing.

The jack snipe is a *little* smaller and a *lot* less neurotic. It conserves its energy, remaining hidden on the ground until the last possible moment. With care, I can get to within a metre or two, although even at this range, they are far from easy to see. The back of a jack snipe has pale straw-coloured lines running across it. They break up its outline and look *exactly* like the dead, yellowing stems of the moor-grass that grows all around this pool. A bird might be there, *right there*, just a few feet ahead, but without meticulous, pixel-by-pixel scrutiny of the scene, the image fails to coalesce within the human eye. Still, it's a game I play occasionally, and if successful I can watch the bird with binoculars in dragonfly mode, set at their minimum focusing distance. Jack snipe are restrained and inexpressive even when they finally decide to move. Their response feels more proportionate to the minimal threat that I pose. There are no disgruntled calls, the escape flight is low and straight, and the bird flops back down into cover within 100 metres or so, rather than careening away into the far distance.

If it's late in the day I'll head home along the forest road. It's longer but less treacherous than the route through the clearing, especially in the fading light. And there is another advantage: it gives me an excellent chance of catching up with the final bird in the trio of long, straight-billed waders that use these hills. The 'snipe of the woods' is another master of camouflage: it might as well be made of leaf litter. Its response to approaching humans borrows a little from each of its relatives. Like the jack snipe, it often sits tight until the last minute. But when it thinks it has been spotted (and, in my case, it is *always* wrong) it explodes into the air with a furious clatter of wings, and is out of sight within a few seconds.

Woodcock winter in the damp deciduous wood close to the house, and I sometimes see one bursting out of the trees at dusk, before heading over the garden to spend the night probing the fields for worms. But it makes good use of the hills, too, hiding out during the day at the edges of plantations, or on slopes of bracken and heather, before flying into the glen to feed as the light fades. It is a solitary, largely nocturnal bird, seen in ones and twos (if it is seen at all), in contrast to the habitually flocking waders down on the mudflats. People are usually surprised to learn that this is our most abundant wintering wader. Its secret is its flexibility. Thinly spread it may be, but it makes use of vast areas of woods, plantations, moors and farmland.

At rest, the woodcock is invisible against its background, but when it wants to be seen it knows just what to do. The undersides of the tips of its tail feathers are white – *very* white. A recent study confirmed that these feather tips represent the most intensely white and reflective plumage so far discovered in any bird.[40] The white tips are hidden most of the time, but when the tail is fanned out, either on the ground or during the spring 'roding' display flights of the males, they reflect what little light is available. I notice it sometimes when I catch a woodcock in the car headlights – flashes of brilliant white standing out from the drab, barely visible browns of the rest of the bird.

* * *

It is in high summer that the draw of the pond is strongest. I come here for the aerial activity at a time of year when watching birds can be frustrating. Although bird populations are peaking now and the countryside is awash with new recruits, those youngsters, inexperienced and vulnerable, tend to keep to cover, and the adults too become less obvious. They sing less frequently now that breeding is almost done for another year, and there isn't the regular toing and froing as food is delivered to hungry nestlings. Many songbirds take the opportunity to moult ahead of their long migration or, if residents, before the onset of colder weather. For a while, without a full set of

---

[40] Dunning, J. et al. (2023) 'How woodcocks produce the most brilliant white plumage patches among the birds.' *Journal of the Royal Society* Vol. 20, Issue 200.

flight feathers, they become easier targets for predators, so it makes sense for them to keep as low a profile as possible.

Thankfully, the heat of summer encourages other things into the air, including a group of animals that depend on water. For the beleaguered birdwatcher the timing is perfect, and this pond is a good place to find them. It attracts a wide range of species, including the specialists that prefer to breed in acidic moorland pools, low in nutrients.

The first of the larger dragonflies to appear is the four-spotted chaser. It has dark patches at the base of the wings, each of which has two dark spots, so that's four in all on either side of the body – hence the name. It flies from the end of May, and the pond supports up to a dozen at a time. Short-bodied, lightning-fast and with boundless energy, they zip around above the water and its margins. Apparently, the males are territorial, but to my untrained eye it doesn't seem that way. It looks more like a free-for-all: dragonflies careering randomly around the pond, sparring with each other whenever they happen to meet. By July, numbers have dwindled, or perhaps they have dispersed more widely. Those that remain had better be on their guard. Now they are potential prey as well as predator.

What is Britain's most impressive dragonfly? To my mind, there are two contenders, and this pond is a good place to consider their merits; on a good day, both are here. If long (and well-decorated) abdomens are your thing, then look no further than the beautiful golden-ringed dragonfly. Both sexes have the lovely bands of gold that lend this dragonfly its name, set off perfectly against a dark background, with an extra-long body to accommodate them all. I see these insects mostly along the small, winding burns where they breed, but they pop up here at the pond, too.

The other candidate is the imperious emperor dragonfly. His Royal Highness may be slightly shorter than the golden-ringed dragonfly, but this is a bulkier beast overall, and a fearsome predator at all stages of its lifecycle. The larvae[41] voraciously hunt tadpoles and even small fish. Having emerged as adults, they cruise the margins of the pond with an unmistakable air of authority, preying on flying insects, including

---

41 The larvae are sometimes known as nymphs, though it is hard to imagine anything that behaves less like an Ancient Greek mythological maiden.

butterflies and other dragonflies. The four-spotted chaser is a regular victim, and even the golden-ringed dragonfly can end up as a meal. If we were to settle our question based on combat, there could be only one winner.

In high summer emerald damselflies are common here, resting in their own unique way among the vegetation. Whereas the larger dragonflies rest with their wings fully open, most damselflies, including the delicate, blue-striped azure damselfly that I see here, hold their wings carefully folded away, above the line of the body. Emerald damselflies, however, choose to compromise. They sit with their wings half-open, jutting out at an angle from the body. It's as if they are on perpetual high alert, ready at any second to launch into the air. And yet they spend most of their lives motionless, clinging to the rushes that rise up from the shallow margins. They have less of the aerial dexterity of their larger cousins, but they shine in a different way. Even on a cloudy day, they gleam. The thorax (just behind the head) of the males catches the light most keenly; an oblong of glinting, metallic green, surrounded by soft powder blue, like a carefully mounted jewel.

It took until July of my second summer of visits to stumble upon another eater of insects. I was watching the emerald damselflies doing not very much, as usual, when this predator finally revealed itself. In the absence, these days, of close-focusing eyes, it was my close-focusing binoculars that did the trick as I scanned the muddy edges of the pond for dragonflies. What to the naked eye was an indistinct blur of unremarkable low vegetation resolved into the most perfect little patch of round-leaved sundews. Ever since finding common butterworts – another carnivorous plant – locally, I've been looking out for sundews, suspecting they must be here. That I managed to overlook them for so long in a place I visit often is chastening; another depressing click on the ratchet of declining senses. But no matter; better late than never.

Each plant, I notice, is of a similar size and structure to the butterworts. There's a small, ground-hugging rosette of green leaves, in this case densely coated with reddish hairs, covered, in turn, with the all-important sticky droplets. The tiny white flowers are mounted on central stems about 10–12 centimetres high, in little clusters, the buds heavy enough to cause the tip of each stem to nod down towards the ground.

To make a living in these nutrient-poor soils, sundews feed on the same things as dragonflies. Are the two in direct competition for the limited supply of insects small enough to be caught? Or, rather, is it possible that the plants might even benefit from such a high density of aerial predators? As small flies try to evade the dragonflies, might they seek the cover of low vegetation to hide out for a while, where there is a greater chance of coming to a sticky end? Damselflies provide another, more direct, benefit to the sundews. They are small and delicate enough to fall victim to the sundew's waterside traps. I've yet to find one caught, though a struggling crane fly, flapping helplessly in a futile effort to free itself, showed that the danger is real.

* * *

As the season moves on, a duo of darter dragonflies takes centre stage. Their numbers start to build up when the longest day is already several weeks behind us, just as thoughts are beginning to turn towards autumn. I associate them with August, often the hottest month of the year, as well as with the onset of cooler weather. At the tail-end of the season, in October or even early November, they are usually the only dragonflies still flying.

The black darter is the smaller and scarcer of the two. It is a heathland and moorland specialist. A haunter of acidic pools. I see it only up here in the hills, the males dressed in jet black with just a few, barely noticeable, spots of dull yellow. You wouldn't describe it as pretty, certainly not colourful, but because we have become so used to our dragonflies showing off bold reds, blues, yellows and greens, it has its own unique, understated charm.

Common darters conform more closely to expectations, the males with their familiar red abdomens. They are more common and less fussy about habitat, and they can turn up almost anywhere, zipping about at speeds the human eye struggles to follow. They are delightfully dismissive of humans who stray into their domain. I can remember summer camping trips as a child when darters would line up, dozens at a time, along the guy ropes of our tent and the arms of folding chairs. We tried to catch them, but it was hopeless; the most rapid movement a human can make is, to them, mere clumsy slow motion. It's a superpower, and secure in this knowledge – knowing that escape is easy – they will even land on us, if only we'll stay still for long enough. They make use of me sometimes, when I'm sitting overlooking the pond. We may be the planet's dominant species, but to this dragonfly we are just a handy vantage point from which to survey the surroundings.

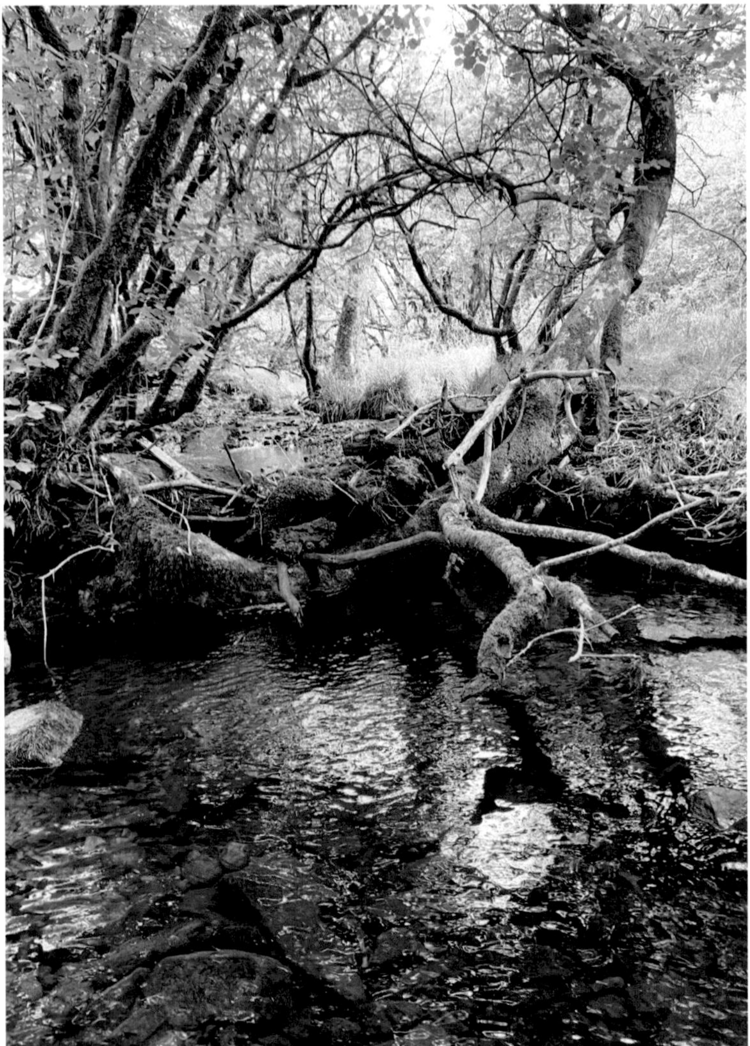

15

The wildwood

Fragments of an ancient landscape and the beating heart of the glen.

'A culture is no better than its woods,' wrote W.H. Auden, capturing an essential truth in remarkably few words.[42] That being so, there is only one place to seek reassurance. Flanking the Hass Burn as it runs below the house are old deciduous woods of ash, hazel, downy birch and alder. They form a backdrop to one side of the garden – lush foliage in summer, a bare framework of branches through the colder months – just one small field away. Birdsong drifts across the space between wood and garden. And after dark the hoots of tawny owls float in through any open window, bringing the ancient sounds of the wildwood into the house.

A two-minute walk takes me inside the wood and away into a wider, wilder world. As with all small woods it appears to expand once entered. It's a trick of the imagination, I think, enabled when familiar sightlines are obscured by vegetation and the mind constructs its own reality for what might lie beyond. Here are old native trees, and every step risks trampling a plant of one kind or another. I'm drawn back here again and again, to the only part of the glen where, hemmed in by foliage, the natural, more-than-human world truly takes centre stage.

For me, and for many other creatures too, these woods are the heart of the glen. Disturb a fox or a roe deer in one of the surrounding fields, and this is where it will run; the fox will head for a gap in the fence

---

[42] This well-known line is from *Bucolics*, a sequence of poems written by Auden in 1952–53. The seven poems in the sequence are Winds, Woods, Mountains, Lakes, Islands, Plains and Streams, and were first published in *The Shield of Achilles* (1955).

– co-opting a run pushed under the lowest wire by badgers – while the deer will leap across, its outline dissolving into the leaves and low branches as it hits the ground on the far side. Hares, too, retreat inside the trees, safe from the whirling blades of the silage machines.

The wood is where the badgers that filch nuts from the patio have their sett. This is where the squirrels build their dreys, and nurture the next generation of garden visitors. This is the only place with trees big enough to hold the young of green woodpeckers, jackdaws and tawny owls, and an understorey thick enough to hide the nests of long-tailed tits and bullfinches. It is where great spotted woodpeckers find dead trees on which to drum out their territorial claims in late winter. And it's where I finally worked out why we get so many honey bees in the garden when I hadn't come across any hives nearby; in the wood one day, alerted by an ominous deep humming from high above me, I found them living wild, in a hollowed-out ash tree.

All these creatures venture well beyond the trees in their daily lives but, like me, they always head back to the woods. Auden was right. Whether this tiny fragment would be enough to satisfy him is another matter.

Looking at the maps produced by Guy Shrubsole for his book, *The Lost Rainforests of Britain*, I see that our wood is one of them.[43] To my non-expert eye, it certainly looks and feels like rainforest. Lichens hang from the trees, and ferns sprout from damp, moss-covered branches. Water continues to drip down from the canopy, long after the rain has stopped. Once, the whole glen would have looked like this, the lower reaches at least. This is all that survives.

The oldest and most majestic tree of all – a vast, expanding ash – stands on the boundary of the wood, where there is space for its branches to spread *out* as well as *up*. I've just been to see it, and I took a ball of garden twine. Pinning one end to the deeply fissured bark I stepped carefully around the tree, holding the string tight against the

---

[43] Temperate rainforest is rarer than tropical rainforest. It grows naturally across the western fringes of Britain where levels of rainfall and humidity are sufficiently high. It is a strangely neglected habitat, and although this is starting to change, most of it has already been lost. Before castigating others for the ongoing loss of tropical forests we might pause a while to reflect on our own actions. For a vibrant, engaging account of our rainforests see: Shrubsole, G. (2022) *The Lost Rainforests of Britain*. William Collins, London.

trunk, before cutting it where the ends met. Now, back home, I measure the string, and find that the girth is 4.5 metres. An online converter suggests an age of 239 years for the tree, with a caveat or two about the influence of environmental conditions and different soil types. Let's play safe and say it has been on this spot for two centuries at least. It would have been here before our house was built, and before the iron ore mine now hidden in the woods was conceived. The workers who then toiled there to bring the heavy rock up from beneath the ground would have passed it daily en route to and from the village. Some no doubt would have sheltered beneath it, or sat, as I often do, back against the trunk. I hope it outlives me, but with ash die-back disease now endemic, I'd give it no more than an even chance.

The woods are at their best in late spring. The carpets of bluebells and wild garlic peak in mid-May, beneath a canopy of trees with pristine, newly unfurled leaves. Marsh marigolds add splashes of bright yellow to the wettest places. Early purple orchids and red campions dot pinks and reds into the mix. Resident birds have now been joined by warblers that wintered further south. Blackbirds and song thrushes compete with blackcaps and willow warblers, filling the air with song. The lively, rounded notes of the nuthatch bounce around the woods, fired out in bursts by the only bird able to wander the canopy in all directions; it alone can proceed head-first down a vertical trunk. At this time there is a vibrancy and freshness to the woods, with so much life newly emerged, newly unfurled, newly arrived. Yet there is also a melancholy tinge, because I know it will be another 12 months before this is repeated. Yes, as the summer unfolds there is the promise of better things to come. It's easy to believe. But it's a trick. The woods are already at their finest; the promise is never quite fulfilled.

This is a time when the woods can spring a surprise or two. For me the biggest so far came on a cool day in late April. I was walking the steep slope along the burn, admiring the primroses and the white stars of wood anemones on the far bank, and thinking how poor the butterfly season had been, with only peacock, small tortoiseshell and speckled wood seen so far. Then came a thought-interrupting clatter of wings from the water below. An elongated grey shape lifted into the air and fired itself, arrow-straight, away through the trees, along the line of the burn. Any duck here in the 'not-a-mallard' category is worth a closer look. The shape, the grey body and the contrasting brown head showed that this one was a female goosander, the first I'd seen here.

It's always easier with hindsight, but on looking around it seemed obvious enough why it was here. The old ash trees have holes that might easily provide a secure nest site. And while the burn is only a few feet wide and not deep, its little pools hold plenty of small trout – fish that would now have to be on their guard. This is a bird that any self-respecting ornithologist should have been looking out for all along. And it is another to add to the list of birds present only because this fragment of old woodland is still here.

* * *

Autumn has its own charm, and after the heat and excesses of July and August I'm ready for it. The woods are quieter now. Green is losing its grip as the leaves begin to turn, and plants weaken and collapse to the ground. Every step stirs up the smell of damp leaf litter and decay. But there is no shortage of activity. For many animals this is a time of plenty. The squirrels know this, and they know it won't last. They vanish from the garden, and for the next few weeks, if I want to watch them I must come here to the woods. They are not easy to find, but it's worth the effort; how much better they look scampering wildly through the branches, and feeding on hazelnuts – as they have done for thousands of years – rather than garden handouts shipped in from the tropics.

The woodland nut crop varies from year to year. Our first autumn here was one of abundance. I pulled one branch down for a closer look and was amazed to find a tight cluster of *nine* hazelnuts. So-called 'mast years' are mostly associated with oak and beech trees in Britain, but other trees too vary their production from year to year. If every tree produced a moderate but consistent crop of nuts each year, then most, or all, would be eaten, leaving none to establish new trees. Instead, the crop is poor in some years and wildlife struggles; the populations of animals that depend on the nuts are held in check. Then comes abundance. Now, the animals that managed to make it through the hard times can't keep up. The nuthatches, jays, woodpeckers, squirrels, mice and voles eat and hide what they can, yet still there is more. The trees benefit from this excess – and, as it happens, so do the humans that live in the house nearby.

This is sometimes portrayed as a cooperative venture by the trees; a carefully planned strategy. Far more likely, it is governed mostly by environmental conditions that affect the production and development of the nuts. But any tree out of step will be at a disadvantage, so there is evolutionary pressure to conform. Produce a bumper crop when your neighbours have little to offer, and ravenous seekers of nuts will be drawn in from afar and will consume the lot; produce nothing in a good year and an opportunity to reproduce will have been missed. Lean years are normal, though that doesn't stop people fretting about why their favourite garden tree has once again failed to produce any nuts. This is a frequent question on gardening programmes, and as Ken Thompson points out in his book *Common or Garden*, 'it never gets a sensible answer. You need to ask an ecologist, not a gardener.'[44]

In a good year we don't feel guilty about harvesting hazelnuts. As I walk the woods I pick them casually, taking advantage of the hazel's flexibility, and bending branches down to bring them within reach. Those that fall or slip easily from their green cases when given a gentle squeeze are worth taking. (My dad, brought up in rural Gloucestershire, calls them 'slippers'.) Back home I lay them out on the kitchen table so they can dry out and finish ripening. Stored in tins they will last until the following autumn and beyond, and the taste will only mature and sweeten with age.

We feed some of these nuts to the squirrels through the winter. At first I wondered if they might be disconcerted by this sudden, unseasonal appearance a long way from the nearest tree, but of course that's not how it works. Wild animals have no time to ponder such inconsistencies. Instinct kicks in, and each nut is either skilfully shelled and consumed or squirrelled away for later. We regularly find new hazel saplings in the flowerbeds, the nuts long forgotten by the animal that planted them.

---

44 Thompson, K. (2023) *Common or Garden: Encounters with Britain's 50 Most Successful Wild Plants*. Profile Books, London.

Any nuts left on the patio are dealt with by the evening badger patrol, though they have none of the squirrels' dexterity or patience. Every night – and it really is *every* night – they amble across the field from the wood and up the steps to the small patio outside the lounge. If they arrive when the light is still good, we might pause the TV and watch for a while. If it's dark, Hazel, with better ears than mine, knows they've arrived by the crunching sound audible through the glass doors. Up to five animals at a time jostle for position, hoovering up food with ruthless efficiency and turning hazelnuts into a litter of shell fragments. No doubt they do the same thing in the autumn woods where the evidence is all but invisible among the decaying leaves.

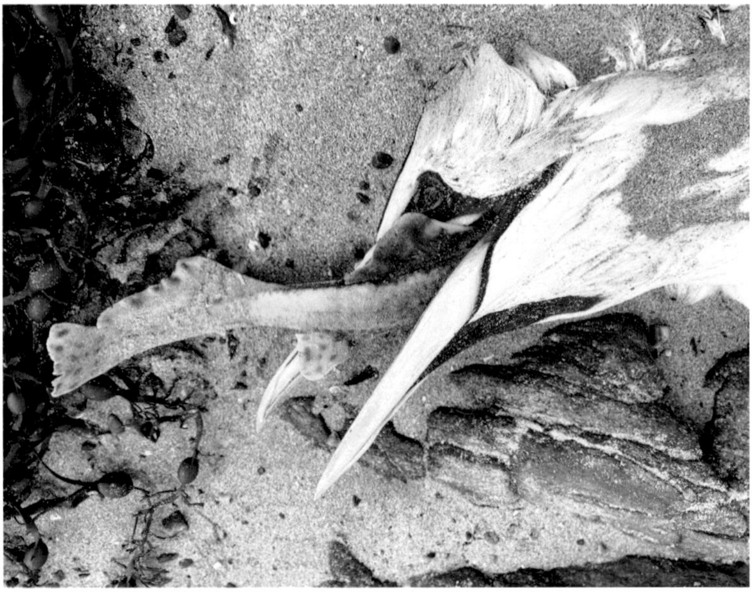

16

Wildwater

Intertidal mud and merse; a shark, killed by a gannet, killed by a shark (and found by a dog) – everything interconnected and 'hitched to everything else in the universe'.

The small bay just beyond Auchencairn is dominated by an area of intertidal mudflats, backed by saltmarsh, a reedbed fringed with scrubby bushes and a low, stony beach. I say 'small' because it looks that way on the map; it's a tiny rectangular indentation on the northern edge of the vast Solway Firth. But for a leisurely walk around it, I'll need to set aside half a day at least.

I'm not especially drawn to estuary birdwatching, so I don't come here too often. Why is that? There are a few reasons, I think. This is the only place in the glen where I'm unlikely to be alone; it's close to the village, and people use the beach for exercise or dog walking. It also lacks the potential for genuine exploration. Everything is visible here, all at once. There are no corners to wander round, hills to scramble up, or groups of trees to navigate to see what might be on the other side. Here there is only merse and mud, flat and exposed, stretching away towards the horizon. But each to their own; for others, these are the things that give estuaries their special appeal. There's a chance of bumping into someone for a friendly chat or to compare birding notes. And there's no need to wander great distances; all the birds are there, laid out in full view, waiting to be identified. If something exciting happens out on the mudflats – a peregrine on the hunt for a victim perhaps – there is little chance of missing out on the action.

Before I finish grumbling, there's one final drawback if you are on foot. To watch birds here, scattered as they are across acreages of mud, a telescope is essential. It's heavy to lug around, and on a cold day, fiddling with the steel legs of the tripod numbs the fingers. In warmer, sunny weather there is heat haze to contend with, and views of birds are often hard-won and blurred by the distance and the thick, heavy air. Still, while some coast-loving birds wander up to the fields or ponds closer to the house, or pass through the glen on their way to and from the coast, others are only available here. If I want to watch wigeon, shelduck and a varied assortment of waders, each with a subtly different way of pulling food from the mud, this is the place. So I come to check in on them every so often, especially in spring and autumn when birds are on the move and there is more chance of a surprise.

As with the nearby seabird cliffs, the top end of the bay is an SSSI,[45] protecting the saltmarsh and mudflats, and the birds that make use of them. Using NatureScot's website it's easy to find documents online that describe the site and summarise the way it's managed.[46] It's news to me that wildfowling is permitted – or perhaps *was* permitted, given that the documents are a little dated. I learn, too, about the presence of common cordgrass, a non-native hybrid that can grow across mudflats and deprive waterbirds of valuable feeding areas.[47]

The SSSI documents also mention fishing. This we *do* already know about, thanks to our accident-prone spaniel and because I often see fishermen on the rocks near Balcary Point. In spring, when distracted from the seabird activity offshore, I've watched them though the telescope, pulling up dogfish and the strange-looking thornback rays that are common in this part of the Solway, with flattened, kite-shaped bodies and long spiky tails.

But back to the dog. Wandering along the beach one morning she sniffed out a decomposing fish on the strandline. There followed the usual battle between animal – delighted at this unexpected meal – and human, concerned with the appalling smell and potential for vomit-stained carpet. But in trying to separate dog from 'food' there was a problem. A steel fish-hook, once lodged within the fish, was now

---

45 Site of Special Scientific Interest. They were legally established by an Act of Parliament in 1949, and now there are over 5,000 of them in Britain.
46 See: https://sitelink.nature.scot/map (nature.scot)
47 Common cordgrass *Sporobolus anglicus* (formerly *Spartina anglica*) is a hybrid arising from the native small cordgrass and the introduced American smooth cordgrass.

stuck firmly in the dog's jowls, still attached to line that disappeared into a tangle of washed-up seaweed. The hook was fully 7 centimetres long; if you wanted something about the right size to reel in a cocker spaniel, this would do. Fishing line is designed not to break, but Hazel eventually managed to bite through it, leaving hook and a short length of nylon still in place. Attempts to ease the hook free resulted in frantic head thrashing and pitiful yowls of protest. There was only one option: a drive to Castle Douglas, a dose of sedatives (for the dog – though by now I would have welcomed them) and a vet patient enough to cut through the shaft of the hook before carefully extracting it. 'Take your fishing tackle home,' I shouted on Twitter as we waited in the car, though of course it wouldn't have been discarded deliberately.

A few years ago, further up the west coast, on Mull, our dog made an altogether more interesting tideline discovery. Dead gannets are not an especially unusual find and occasionally they wash up along the shores of the Solway. They are always impressive when seen close up, with their huge wings – think albatross but broader – and the strange, otherworldly blue-green lines on their feet. But in this case, it wasn't the bird that had attracted the dog; it was the thing protruding 15 centimetres beyond its open beak – the body and tail of a dogfish.[48] These small sharks have broad heads and a distinctive rough skin that feels like sandpaper. It is not a fish designed to slip easily down a bird's throat, unlike the gannet's more typical prey of herring or mackerel. The dogfish was wedged firmly in place, resisting all canine and human attempts to dislodge it. Two bodies in the same spot, each animal losing its life in a very different way. Cause of death: 'choked on shark' or 'partially swallowed by gannet', depending on your point of view.

It was a strange sight, and the more I thought about it, an unlikely pairing. Gannets, patrolling above the waves, hunt for fish near the surface. The dogfish, though, is a creature of the depths. It makes its living by scavenging along the bottom, safely out of reach of aerial predators. I've heard that dogfish are often discarded from fishing boats by skippers seeking more highly valued fish. Most likely then,

---

48 The lesser spotted dogfish *Scyliorhinus canicula*, our commonest species, is most likely the one involved here.

our bird was scavenging behind a fishing boat, as they often do, in the hope of an easy meal. The gannet lends its name to voracious human feeding behaviour on account of its apparent greed – devouring whole fish in one go (or trying to). According to my favourite sea-fishing book, the dogfish has an attitude that is not dissimilar; it hunts in packs, driven by a 'rabid hunger and terrible table manners … a doggie will bite chunks out of a whole dead dolphin if it needs to.'[49] A sorry stalemate between these two gluttonous species was perhaps the inevitable outcome.

* * *

A late March walk to the coast was inspired by stumbling across a local tide timetable online. By chance, one of the year's highest tides was predicted for the following day, with a peak around lunchtime. I arrived in good time, to find that the bay was already full to the brim with water. The scrubby reedbed above the shoreline was partly submerged and low waves were breaking through it, each one pushing the water level at my feet a little higher. For at least one resident of the rough grassland above the shore it was all too much. Field voles were being flooded out of their nests as I watched. One shuffled away from the edge of the water in front of me, brushing against my boot as it headed for drier ground. I saw another do the same thing a few metres away, and then a sharp-eyed carrion crow revealed that not all had been so lucky. It flew down to the edge of the reeds, and plucked a bedraggled, short-tailed body from the water. It started to eat it, resting on a floating log, but when buffeted by the next wave it headed away inland, carrying its meal.

Toads are better placed than voles to cope with inundation, but they too were being displaced. I found one crawling through thick grass just above the waterline, and out over the water another carrion crow was searching for more casualties. It picked up what I had assumed would be another vole, until flailing amphibious limbs became apparent, dangling beneath the crow's beak.

---

[49] Fisher, N. (2010) *The River Cottage Sea Fishing Handbook*. Bloomsbury, London.

Birds have no such problems. They can move away as the water covers the mud, though being deprived of their favoured feeding grounds for a few hours is no small inconvenience. High tide is not helpful for estuary birds, though it can be a good time for us to watch them as they are pushed higher up the shore, ever closer to an astutely positioned observer. But when the tide covers everything, as today, birds are forced out of the bay entirely and onto the fields above. Sixty or so curlews were probing hopefully at the damp soil of a grass field. A few weeks from now, most will have moved on to their breeding grounds inland. Then they will be outnumbered for a while by their diminutive, stripy-faced cousins, whimbrels, passing through en route to Iceland or Scandinavia.

In the same field as the curlew, a little egret picked its way across a patch of waterlogged ground. Shelduck were also present in numbers. They don't have the tools that the waders and egrets use to feed in damp pasture, so they were sitting out the tide – stationary white blobs, resting incongruously in the lush grass in pairs and trios. At a distance, with nothing for scale, I might have taken them for sheep, chewing the cud before their next bout of grazing. When the tide turns, the shelduck will spring back to life and fly out into the bay to resume their endless sifting of the mud for tiny snails.

For a few waterbirds the incoming water *creates* feeding opportunities rather than ruining them. Fish move in with the tide, and I watched as a cormorant, with its white, breeding season thigh-patch, tried its luck. Lesser black-backs and herring gulls were resting on the sea, flying up every so often to patrol a stretch of water, on the lookout for edible morsels washed in with the tide. Gulls, adaptable as ever, can find food at any time.

As I waded through water a foot deep on the coast path, it was clear that conditions for landbirds had changed too. An immaculate male stonechat was perched on top of a low bush, firing off its distinctive calls like an old-fashioned camera shutter clicking open, then shut again. Is there any bird more helpful when it comes to allowing itself to be watched? It's as if they are aware of their striking plumage and want to show it off. That's not it, of course; they perch in prominent places so they can survey their surroundings. With its large, dark eyes the stonechat is a visual hunter, scanning the ground below for movements. Only here now, there was no ground to scan, just water, and so the bird clung stoically to its perch as I walked by. Perhaps, as the tide receded, there would be a bonanza of displaced, dying invertebrates that would be easy to catch. And perhaps that's just what it was waiting for?

Another bird was acting now rather than waiting. A lone meadow pipit, deprived of its familiar grassland habitat, was foraging offshore, picking its way delicately across a floating island made from seaweed, bits of dead reed-stem and other detritus. Light and nimble on its toes, it was able to keep its feet dry, as its temporary feeding place rolled upwards, then back down, with each incoming wave. It's possible it was eating seeds, but I suspect it was picking off invertebrates that had been washed from their resting places in the reedbed and rough grass, and become mixed up with all the plant debris.

A prior engagement meant I couldn't stay to watch the water drain back out of the bay, although it was already beginning its journey. I promised myself I'd return in the summer. And on a calm, warm day in early August, I'll pick my way across the hundreds of little islands of saltmarsh that now are hidden beneath the waves. I'll hop across from one to the next, over the deep gullies of mud and stones carved out by the sea, enjoying the soft purple haze from thousands of sea-lavender plants. It will feel like a very different place.

On the walk home I found myself thinking of John Muir, of all people, as I tried to recall his words about interconnectedness; that 'when we try to pick out anything by itself, we find it hitched to everything else in the universe'.[50] It's not a contentious view. You might say, after a moment's reflection, that it's a statement of the blindingly obvious. But the words are so beautifully conceived they somehow add meaning, or at least clarity of thought, about the way the world works. He was writing about the wilderness of what is now the Yosemite National Park in California. But it's true also of a small bay at the edge of the Solway, as the water levels rise unusually high. At once there are animals pushed out of their homes, new ones arriving, and species adapting – or failing to adapt – to the changing conditions. For every

---

50 Muir, J. (1911) *My First Summer in the Sierra*. Canongate Books, Edinburgh (2014 edition).

struggling creature another one benefits, and the winners and losers are hitched intimately to each other and to their environment. The position of the Moon relative to the Earth, the incoming sea, the floundering voles and invertebrates, the carrion crows, stonechats and meadow pipits; all are hitched together, interconnected and inseparable.

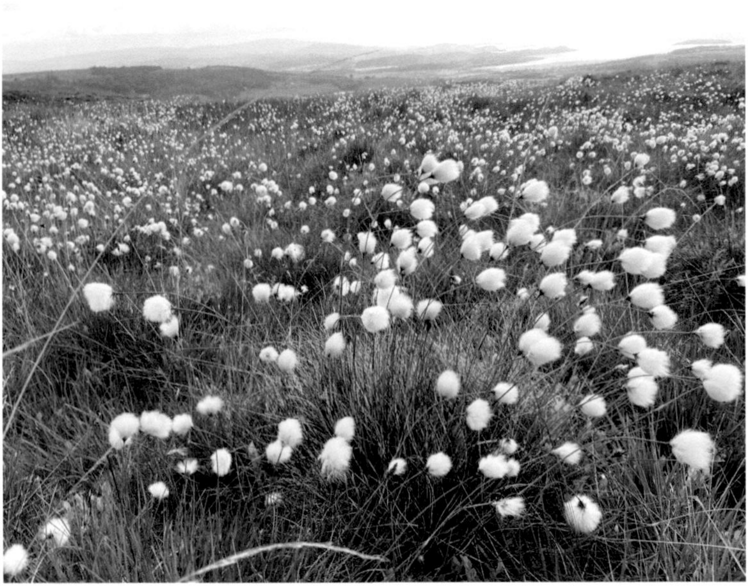

17

Time well spent

Away in the hills – and the benefits of time apart from humanity. 'We come from the earth and therefore, rather unsurprisingly, we have a connection to it. Denying that connection is akin to self-harm.'[51]

An interest in wildlife can, if you're not careful, turn into a mini-industry, with walks carefully planned, and every plant and animal scrutinised, identified and recorded for posterity – on the walk itself if you have a smartphone. Pockets fill with bits of kit and reference books to help get to grips with troublesome specimens. Images are taken, and an app on your phone can tell you what it thinks you have seen. Increasingly often, as the software develops, it will be right.

Gathering information helps to demonstrate the value of a place and the importance of protecting it. But it can have a downside too. Identifying and recording other species is often about imposing control, bringing nature under *our* spell, and trying to work out how much value *we* should place upon it. This, then, helps perpetuate the myth that we are apart from, and superior to, the rest of the natural world. And it can drain some of the magic that comes from spending time in nature and feeling that we are a meaningful part of it, with no fixed agenda and no human-orientated task to complete.

That's my excuse, anyway. I can put a name to a bird, and to most butterflies and dragonflies. I'm good with trees and getting better with wild flowers, but I lack the dedication required to properly get to grips with the more obscure and challenging groups of plants and

---

[51] Fitton, J.A. (2023) *Hermit: A Memoir of Finding Freedom in a Wild Place*. Hutchinson Heinemann, London.

invertebrates. Even with birds, I don't take the identification process too far. An autumn wheatear is just that. Unless it looks obviously different, I'm not going to work studiously through every feature just to make sure it's not one of the rarer species. A flock of gulls in a winter field is a welcome spectacle rather than an invitation to pick through every bird in turn in the hope of finding something unusual. The subtleties of size, shape and plumage that lead some birders to Caspian gulls and other creatures that didn't exist (or didn't have a name) in my formative years mostly elude me.

I beat myself up sometimes, and succumb to hopeless, short-lived bouts of self-improvement. Recently, I've been trying to get my head around grasses. I've spent hours up in the hills peering at leaf blades, trying to decide whether ligules are pointed or toothed. Are those spikelets awned or unawned? Are they drooping or erect? And what are you supposed to do when the same plant has a mixture of all these things? I've learnt a few new ones. But I haven't got far. It hasn't been fun. And next time I find the same plants, doubtless I'll have forgotten the names anyway.

So it is with the burgeoning array of wildlife monitoring schemes. Too much counting, recording and form-filling eats away at the therapeutic benefits I get from time spent away from the house. Laziness is part of it. But there's more to it than that: what if the joy of being outdoors comes from *escaping* the myriad plans, schemes and relentless ambitions of humanity that already consume so much of our lives?

We find it hard, I think, to shake the idea that everything we do should have a clear purpose. It's a mindset that's worth challenging, and it's one of the few things I've got better at with age. I've become more accepting of knowledge gaps and more relaxed about spending time on my own terms with no firm plan and no itinerary set by others. If identifying and recording is not your thing, then don't feel bad about it; don't turn a life-affirming interest into yet another chore.

* * *

It's with this attitude that I'm setting out today. I have two full days ahead of me and I'll sleep somewhere up in the hills. Binoculars, sleeping bag and bivvy bag excepted, I have no bits of kit, and no books to weigh down my rucksack.

I've also left the map at home. I'm with Charles Foster on this. A map is a powerful representation of human endeavour and control. As he put it, maps are 'literally reductionist: they reduce miles to centimetres, chatty and ineffable woods to splodges of green. And they give us the idea that we can fold up a landscape and stick it in our pocket. The land becomes about us.'[52] I'm reminded of all the surveys I've done when living birds have been captured as two-letter codes, pulled from the wild and rendered in pencil on a map. These days, our phones offer a yet more powerful symbol of human control: an instant map of *everywhere* (your own location conveniently centred as you walk) as well as an instant connection back to the world you are trying to walk away from. I leave my phone at home too.

I start along the track from the house still undecided about which side of the glen to cross to get up into the hills. But over the ridge to my left a pair of ravens are embroiled in a noisy aerial battle with a red kite. I turn that way so I can continue to watch them as I walk up and away from the farm.

Having climbed over the uppermost stone dyke, I head towards the ancient, lonely ruins of Suie Hillfort. I've not been there for a while, and with views in all directions it'll be a good place to plan where to go next. The walking isn't easy, as the moorland here includes damp, boggy areas intimately mixed with drier, safer ground. Bracken is a good plant to hold close to in this situation, as it favours well-drained soils. In contrast, the wetter slopes and depressions come with warning lights in the form of white tufts of cottongrass, and there are the dry stems and flowerheads from last year's bog asphodels. Later in the summer the new plants will produce fiery yellow flower spikes, cooling to orange as the fruits develop.

Scanning ahead to work out a viable route, I recall the words of Donald Watson, the famous naturalist, author and painter of birds. He lived in Galloway, a little further inland from here, and he likened the

---

[52] Foster, C. (2021) *Being a Human: Adventures in 40,000 Years of Consciousness*. Profile Books, London.

colours and textures of one of his local hills to that of a fruit cake.[53] I thought it a strange choice of words, but he had an artist's eye and now I can see just what he meant. There are the old, straw-coloured leaves from last year's moor-grass, and areas of faded, orange-brown bracken – this year's green fiddlehead shoots beginning to push up through the litter. Little islands of heather form darker patches (the currants?); and outcrops of pale rock, textured with lichens, complete the effect.

I can find no obvious way around one of the wetter areas. Crossing it, my boots crunch through a tangle of low shrubby bushes which I take to be regenerating willows. Now, though, I'm getting a waft of sweet, resinous air, and I realise my mistake. It's bog myrtle, the soft, orange flowers already past their best, and this year's new leaves beginning to emerge. I pull a few from the plant and rub them between my fingers to release more of the scent, and I'm reminded of times when, under desperate siege from midges, I've used them as an insect repellent, frantically crushing them and wiping the residue across areas of exposed skin. There is, apparently, some science to support this, though I can't say I've ever found it to be effective. This early in the summer, with a bit of a breeze, the area is, for now, midge-free.

The most abundant bird on the moor here is the meadow pipit. I'm watching them more attentively than usual because of something that happened a few days ago. A bird had leapt up from the vegetation under my feet. I had a closer look and there, almost hidden from view, was a small hollow in the side of a tussock of grass, leading to a deep, stunningly well-concealed grassy cup. After more than four decades of watching meadow pipits, I'd found my first nest. Today, the bird is teaching me about the powerful benefits of 'getting your eye in'. I notice one fly up a few metres ahead. Two days ago I would have thought nothing of it. But now I mark the spot and step carefully towards it. There are two thick tussocks of grass close together. And when I peer down closely, inside one of them is the nest.

The only vaguely taxing task of the day comes later in the evening, after hours of aimless yet mindful wandering through the hills. I have many square miles of uninhabited, infrastructure-free land to choose

---

53 Watson, D. (1973) 'Mountain and Moorland' in *Birdwatchers' Year*. Poyser, Berkhamsted.

from, but still, finding a place to sleep is never easy. The ideal spot should be sheltered, flat, not too hard, free of stones and holes (and snakes). Ideally it should come with a decent view and be close to a burn. Finding such a place can take a while, but it's another mindful endeavour and I know that if I'm too impatient I'll pay the price later. I'm pleased enough, though, with the location I eventually find, and drift off to sleep dimly aware of an unfamiliar bird song, but unable to muster the energy to get up and track it down.

Early the next morning I come round, listening to the same bird. The notes have filtered into my head even before I'm fully awake because my first (semi)conscious thought of the day is: *What on earth is that bird?* Its song is not dissimilar to a blackbird's, but one that is constantly being interrupted. The notes are mostly rich and melodic, with a few more scratchy sections thrown in, too. I struggle to pinpoint singing birds because I rely so much on one good ear. It's a case of turning my head back and forth to work out the direction from which the sound is loudest. It can be a maddening experience, especially, as now, when I'm barely awake and the bird seems to be moving about from one perch to another. Finally, I pin it down. It's a gorgeous male whinchat, the first I've seen locally, orange-flushed breast facing towards me, and the striking black-and-white face turning from side to side as it throws out bursts of song, first one way then the other.

Later that morning I descend from the high moors to a gorse-covered hillside that slopes down to the farmland below. The gorse covers a huge area and the bushes are well over head height, so I'm walking *under* rather than *through* the foliage – stooping and weaving my way between the forest of bare stems. Small patches around the edges have been burnt to try to reclaim some of the grazing, and perhaps that will be the eventual fate of the whole area. For now, though, it creates a sheltered, coconut-infused world, and I'm enjoying the novelty. But escaping from it, as I near the bottom of the slope, is another matter. Although there are sheep trails running in all directions it's hard to know which one to pick, and with all the spikey foliage they are of limited use for a tall, soft-bodied human. I come across a long-dead sheep and wonder if it too had struggled to find its way out. The bones are strewn across a surprisingly wide area, and must have kept the local scavengers well fed as they pulled it apart.

I finally find my way back into the light, arms dripping with sweat and a little blood. I follow the burn which runs back down into the glen, relishing the sun on my arms and the fact that the view is no longer constrained by a 360-degree wall of gorse. The burn here is flanked by a narrow strip of old woodland, mostly downy birches, clinging to steep, uneven banks. I can see these trees from the garden. In winter they give off a distinctive hazy purple glow due to the colour of the bark on the young birch twigs, an effect that dissolves imperceptibly as I walk towards the trees.

This fragment of woodland is ancient. But it's accessible to livestock – sheep, and sometimes cattle – so is on borrowed time. There are no young trees coming through to replace those nearing the end of their lives; the animals see to that. It's a dispiriting situation, but one that adds an extra layer of significance to the place. It's like walking through the ruins of an abandoned village, littered with poignant reminders of its long, rich history, but with little hope for the future. Human nature being what it is, we value things especially highly just as they are taken from us. That's what is happening here; these woods are slipping slowly away, one tree at a time.

* * *

I've picked out a few of the highlights from my time in the hills but they are not important. Not really. It's the time spent away from human infrastructure that I value. Back at home, I've been trying to think through the reasons why sleeping out for even a night or two can be such a powerful experience, and reading what others have had to say about it.

In his ground-breaking book *Reconnection* Miles Richardson pointed out that we have engaged with the rest of the natural world on equal terms for over 90 per cent of our existence.[54] As hunter-gatherers we were part of the fabric of the landscape, keenly attuned to the

---

54 Richardson, M. (2023) *Reconnection: Fixing our Broken Relationship with Nature.* Pelagic Publishing, London.

animals and plants around us, and dependent upon them to stay alive. We wouldn't have seen ourselves as apart from, or superior to, the rest of nature, and we didn't live by trying to bring it under our control. Our brains are still wired that way, if only we can step away from the constraints of modern living for long enough to take advantage.

It's easy enough to find awe-inspiring birds and scenery without straying much from roads or well-used paths, and with no need to stay out overnight. And yet the deeper connections come, I think, from spending more than just a few snatched hours in semi-wild places, and from getting as far away as possible from human infrastructure. Exploring human-dominated landscapes involves following well-established routes, binding ourselves to the will of others and sticking rigidly to within a few feet of lines marked out for us to follow. Escaping from these limitations is liberating. Jay Griffiths was typically emphatic when reflecting on her need for regular trips to wild places, and she recognised that these feelings are probably there, somewhere, in us all:

> I was, in fact, homesick for wildness, and when I found it I knew how intimately – how resonantly – I belonged there. We are charged with this. All of us. For the human spirit has a primal allegiance to wildness.[55]

One way of trying to explain this 'allegiance to wildness' is the concept of thin places. It is said that in wilder, more remote, spots the boundary between the world we know and everything else is more porous. In those places it's easier, so the argument goes, to peek through the veil from our world to the others beyond that we little understand. Even for the non-religious, a spiritual element is often part of the explanation; our feelings of awe and reverence appear to transcend the reality of our own mundane existence.

I understand the temptation to think that way. But I don't think there is any need to invoke the supernatural; surely it is simpler than that. Out in the hills, my senses are sharpened and awareness of my surroundings enhanced because I'm more tuned into the way we all

---

55 Griffiths, J. (2006) *Wild: An Elemental Journey*. Penguin Books, London.

once lived. There is no guidance from wider humanity to help decide where to go next, to pick out a viable route through the landscape, or to find a place to sleep that's warm and comfortable. These are tiny things. But we have evolved to take them seriously, and our minds adapt quickly to these new circumstances. When we are away from other people and the prescribed lines and strictures of humanity, we regain sole responsibility for ourselves. It is, then, hardly surprising that we stop fretting about matters beyond our control and start to pay closer attention to the things we can see, hear and smell.

Marc Hamer hints at this by suggesting that time spent alone is a way of escaping from ourselves as much as from others, or at least the version of ourselves that we must usually live with:

> Any experienced solo hiker ... knows the feeling of power that nature has when we silence ourselves. Go into the wild alone, away from human company or phone signals for a decent length of time ... and the awareness of that power is inescapable, unavoidable, impossible to ignore. It can dominate your thoughts ... heighten your senses so that you feel it with your skin and hair ... Tiny sounds, tiny smells, tiny sensations will grab your unwilling flesh, push you around and tell you who you are.[56]

The writer, John Fowles, found a unique joy in exploring a landscape free of other people as a child, one that had a huge influence on his future novels. In *The Tree* he describes his move to rural Devon (my old stomping ground) as an evacuee from London during the Second World War. Having escaped suburbia, he revels in what he calls the 'unpeopled secrecy of the Devon countryside':

> I was really addicting myself, and beyond curability, to the pleasures of discovery, and in particular of isolated discovery and experience. The lonelier the place, the better it pleased me: its silence, its aura ... such 'lost'

---
56 Hamer, M. (2023) *Spring Rain*. Harvill Secker, Milton Keynes.

valleys still existed and in some of them the rest of the world did not. But of course they were finite, and at some point ended at a lane, a cottage or farmhouse, 'civilization'; and discovery died.[57]

The idea of 'thin places' misses the point, for me anyway. The opposite is true. Far from peeking behind the veil to glimpse another world, the time I spend in the hills is about becoming more fully immersed in the realities of this one, and appreciating all that it has to offer; time spent looking out into the surroundings and seeing them clearly, rather than plodding along a fixed route, pondering life's problems and fretting about unsettling world events over which I have no influence. Wild places, away from distractions, might *feel* like another world, but that's only because our usual day-to-day experience is so sanitised and prescribed, so very far away from our origins.

To reconnect takes time. If I'd had longer than two days, no doubt the experience would have been richer still. As Nan Shepherd put it, the senses take a while to adjust and only then 'the eye sees what it didn't see before, or sees in a new way what it had already seen.' For her, the moments of strongest connection when exploring the Cairngorms were unpredictable but 'they come to me most often […] waking out of outdoor sleep [or] after hours of steady walking'.[58] For most of us, an hour or two away from the routines of normal life may be all that is typically available. It is time well spent. But the more time that I can set aside for this, the better I become. As Jay Griffiths said so clearly, I think the same is true for all of us.

---

57 Fowles, J. (1979) *The Tree*. Aurum Press, London.
58 Shepherd, N. (1977) *The Living Mountain*. Aberdeen University Press, Aberdeen.

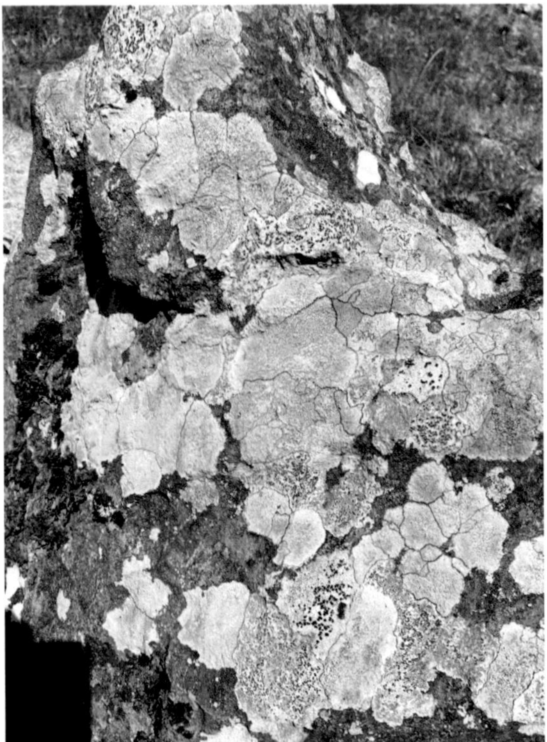

18

End notes

A stubborn paradox, and trying to stay cheerful despite everything.

And what is Life? – An hour-glass on the run,
A Mist retreating from the morning sun,
A busy, bustling, still repeated dream;
Its length? A minute's pause, a moment's thought;
And Happiness? – A bubble on the stream,
That in the act of seizing shrinks to nought.

John Clare[59]

Over recent years it has become customary in a book about wildlife to finish on a note of despondency; to offer a few personal thoughts and ideas as we slump, ever more surely, into the twin, interlinked crises afflicting biodiversity and the climate. I've touched on some of the issues in this book but I've avoided addressing them head-on. Partly, I think, that's down to self-preservation, in that dwelling too much on relentless loss and decline would turn something that brings joy into a source of grief and despair. Then there's the delicate matter of guilt. I'm as much a part of the problem as anyone else, and that's a tough thing to have to acknowledge.

It took a bird to remind me how much our perceptions of the world vary with state of mind and recent experience. I was out in the garden,

---

[59] As a long-time fan of John Clare I was surprised that I'd not come across this poem before seeing it quoted in Hamer, M. (2021) *Seed to Dust: A Gardener's Story*. Harvill Secker, London.

belatedly putting in a few potatoes. A cuckoo had been with me all morning, singing from across the glen almost non-stop. During our five years in mid-Devon this sound had been hard to come by, and on the rare occasions I heard a cuckoo it was always a joyful, uplifting experience. But here in south-west Scotland they are faring better. Around our house the sound has become – and I hesitate to say it – almost monotonous.

Focused on the potatoes, I must have tuned it out after a while. I became aware of it again only when it started to sing a variation on its usual theme, inserting an extra note into each phrase, as cuckoos sometimes do: 'cuck-*cuck*-oo, cuck-*cuck*-oo'. A car we hired recently had the same trick. Leave the seatbelt unfastened, and a gentle warning ping started up to remind you of your carelessness. But if it was ignored for too long, its pitch and urgency increased as if, like the cuckoo, it was insisting upon your attention.

Life is like that, I suppose. Our state of mind is fickle, and the way we think about the wildlife around us is not fixed. We all have 'glass half full' and 'glass half empty' days, or even moments within a day, influenced by mood as well as events. Cuckoos can bring overwhelming joy, or they can slip, unnoticed, into the background. When it comes to issues far bigger than an appreciation of bird song, our capricious minds are no bad thing. Relentless positivity is not always helpful; it can be achieved only by turning a blind eye to some of the grievous harms we are inflicting on our world. But sinking into perpetual despair is no good either. Changes in behaviour can only happen if we feel there are things worth saving and progress is achievable – if there is at least some hope for the future. We must, somehow, find the right balance between hope and despair.

* * *

My wildlife watching, these days, is focused on our glen, and mostly I cover the ground on foot. I'm very much a 'low carbon birder', to borrow the title of Javier Caletrío's inspiring book.[60] But I still make

---

60 Caletrío, J. (2022) *Low Carbon Birding*. Pelagic Publishing, London.

a few long-distance trips by car, and in the past, I've done plenty of travelling around Britain as well as further afield. Over the years I've burnt more than my fair share of carbon. Stephen Rutt summed things up in his thoughtful book *The Eternal Season*, talking of 'the paradox of how we manage to be simultaneously aware of climate change and yet live our lives without responding to it.'[61] He's right. Even as I concern myself with the biodiversity and climate crisis, I'm still contributing to the problem.

We have all, it seems, become experts at making allowances for our own excesses while simultaneously objecting to the excesses of others. In the past I justified my carbon emissions because they were needed for work, to see family or even to write a book. The excuses extended to fun trips abroad to watch wildlife; these provided money for local communities and an incentive to protect important wildlife habitats. Business travellers, meanwhile, point out that jetting around the globe helps bring economic benefits and employment to those who desperately need it. There is so often, it seems, a good reason why *you* are the exception and *everyone else* is the rule.

Another example. A few years ago, I drove from Devon to the Somerset Levels for a day's birding at Shapwick Heath. En route I learnt of Donald Trump's intention to open up new areas for oil exploration within an Alaskan national park. In the same news bulletin there was a story about a contentious sponsorship deal between a London art gallery and a major oil company. I tutted and shook my head in despair; I knew where I stood on these issues, even as I motored along the M5 to watch birds. Before returning home, I filled up the car. I don't remember, but it's entirely possible I used a petrol station run by the company sponsoring the art gallery. Only later did I even consider the irony. A non-essential, fun day out. Another voluntary contribution to climate change. Grumbling to myself about the behaviour of oil companies at the same time as buying their product.

It is an unavoidable truth that individual sacrifices reduce impacts by such a miniscule amount that they make no measurable difference. At the same time, the well-being of the individual is impacted greatly.

---

61 Rutt, S. (2021) *The Eternal Season: Ghosts of Summers Past, Present and Future*. Elliott & Thomson, London.

This is the underlying essence of Stephen Rutt's paradox. We visit beautiful places and complain that tourists are spoiling them. We eat unsustainable foods (or feed them to garden birds) and rail against the destruction and overexploitation of wildlife habitats. We are affronted when an oil company sponsors an art exhibition, but we'll happily buy their fuel. If lots of people made significant lifestyle changes then that *would* make a difference. But that doesn't carry much weight when it comes to deciding on an individual course of action.

We should all try to do better, of course. Governments *must* do better. I don't have any inspiring new suggestions beyond that. All I can offer here is the coping mechanism that helps me, just a little, when despair threatens to take over. If I start to fret about the future then I make myself think about the planet in terms of long timescales. It's the deep time equivalent of staring into the night sky and marvelling at our insignificance. We often hear that we are 'wrecking the planet' – but the planet will be okay. It has already been through five mass extinctions caused by natural events. Humans are just one creature among many, and so the next extinction event will be natural too. After each event, the dominant forms of life are lost, or radically reduced, and a new world order emerges, very different to what was there before. Whatever we do (or don't do) in the coming decades, this will happen again, many times.

Author and commentator Peter Marren wrote about extinction, and he too managed to retain a level of optimism, despite concluding that it would be impossible to avoid a sixth major planetary event.[62] We can't prevent it, he observed, because we are already living through it. On a personal level, he notes that it is 'too big to comprehend; monstrous, unforgivable but ultimately unfathomable'. The only option we have left is to 'enjoy things as they are, not what they were, or what they might come to be.'

One day, creatures impossible for us to imagine will sift through the deposits we have left behind and attempt to make sense of them. They will piece together a story from our bones and those of our livestock, the layers of tarmac and concrete, and the uncountable multi-coloured

---

[62] Marren, P. (2022) *After They're Gone: Extinctions Past, Present and Future*. Hodder Studio, London.

fragments of plastic. Considered on a long enough timescale, our actions become all but irrelevant. That's no excuse for complacency and inaction. But, for me anyway, it provides a crumb of comfort. It makes it easier for me to enjoy the wildlife that lives alongside us here in our small corner of Galloway, never mind what might happen in the future. None of us will be here for long. But we *are* here now, and plenty of other species are here with us, despite everything. All we can do is try to enjoy their presence for as long as they remain.

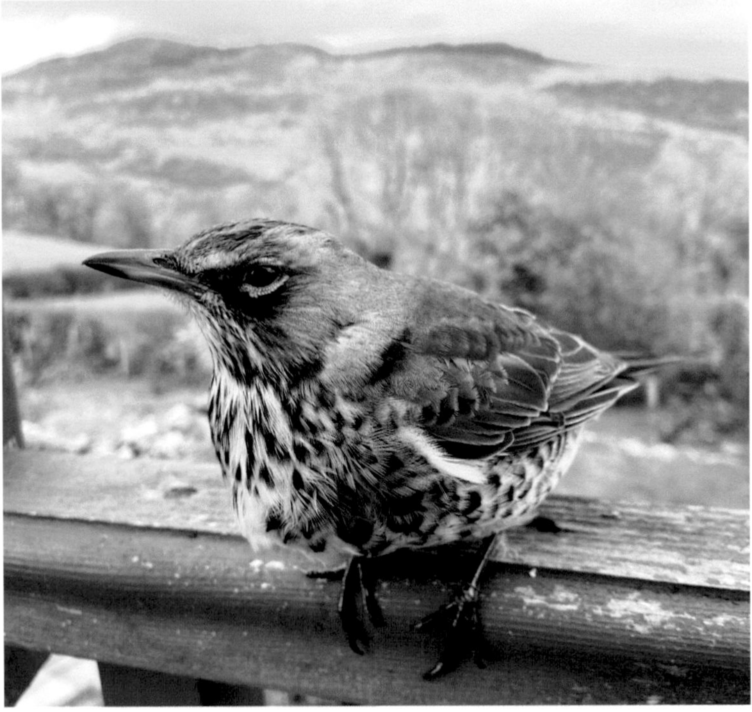

The wildlife

Birdwatchers love a list, so I thought it might be helpful to end with one, and to offer a few words about each of the birds and other animals that I've come across. With a few exceptions (as noted) I've found these species somewhere in the glen, from the high hills around Bengairn, down to the coastal merse and mudflats of Auchencairn Bay and the cliffs at Balcary. The page numbers in brackets show where the birds are mentioned in the text, **bold** indicating more than a passing mention.

I've listed the birds under various categories rather than in strict taxonomic order, which I hope will make them a little easier to find. For example, all the birds of prey and owls are kept together even though they are not closely related; we now know from genetic studies that falcons are more closely related to parrots than they are to any of the other raptors. In similar vein, the swift is placed together with those other highly aerial insect-eating birds, the swallows and martins, even though it is not a near relative.

A few more caveats. Hazel and I are recent arrivals in our corner of Galloway, and the book is about my explorations of the place over our first two years or so rather than a comprehensive survey. Some of the less common or irregular visitors have eluded me up to now: I've not yet come across a turnstone, sanderling, grey plover, short-eared owl or reed warbler, to pick out a few of the more obvious examples. Birds that skulk and have a high-pitched voice may have escaped my attention for a different reason. In the low hills there is plenty of dense, tangled vegetation that looks perfect for grasshopper warblers. They occur regularly in Galloway, so perhaps they come here each spring to hide out among the thick, tussocky grasses and to throw their strange reeling songs into the air. Perhaps. I can no longer hear them so, sadly, I'm none the wiser.

There are some notable absentees among birds associated with freshwater habitats, as my little patch – just one glen, in just one small corner of Galloway

– has nothing bigger than a small burn, a few ponds and several small, reed-fringed lochs. I have yet to find coot, shoveler, gadwall, pintail or pochard locally, though all can be seen easily enough in the wider landscape.

Swans and geese

Mute swan: A few pairs nest on islands in the lochs, and in winter small numbers can be found down in the bay where the merse meets the mudflats.

Whooper swan: Sometimes found in the bay in winter. More rarely, a V of these magical wild swans will fly through the glen in spring or autumn, their long-necked forms and soft, trumpeting calls – 'a constant exchange of snatches of muted brass' as nature writer Jim Crumley put it – casting a brief spell over the place.

Barnacle goose: A delicate, monochrome goose for which the Solway is vitally important as a wintering area, supporting most of the Svalbard breeding population. Smaller than the pink-footed goose, with which it often mixes (though they tend to keep to themselves within the flocks) their return each year is one of the defining features of our autumn. The calls of a large flock lifting up into the air, or from the Vs of birds flighting between their offshore roost site and the coastal fields, can drown out all other sounds. In contrast, the frenetic 'yaps' made by a lone bird remind me of the sort of small, excitable dog that you wouldn't want to live next door to. (5, 98, **123**)

Pink-footed goose: Along with the barnacle geese, they graze the livestock pastures within the lower part of the glen, before heading back to the Solway to roost. Straggling, shape-shifting Vs sometimes pass through the glen, and if I hear them from the house I always step outside. A few weak or injured birds, unable to migrate, remain through the summer. The Greenland race of the white-fronted goose winters not too far away, around Loch Ken, so I keep a hopeful eye out, but with no luck so far. (5, **100**, **123**)

Canada goose: Small numbers are present all year. A few pairs nest on the lochs and ponds, wherever there are small islands to provide protection from foxes and other predators. (135)

The wildlife

Greylag goose: A resident in low numbers, though with their loud, inharmonious calls, they are impossible to miss. They breed around the lochs, but nests are not always close to water. I found one sitting on eggs in a bracken patch high up in the hills. Another time I watched a mother leading small goslings though grassland and scrub down towards the beach. (**92–3**)

Ducks, crakes and rails

Shelduck: Common in the bay for much of the year, though they become harder to find in summer when most British shelduck head eastwards across the North Sea for their annual moult. In winter, dozens are often dotted about across the mudflats, their large size and pale plumage making them easy to pick out as they filter tiny estuarine snails from the mud. (142, **155**)

Teal: A delightful, diminutive duck that occasionally springs up from one of the ponds in the hills should I stray too close. It is more reliably seen on the small lochs where up to 100 can be found together in winter, dipping in and out of the fringing vegetation, chirruping to each other constantly as if for reassurance. (135)

Wigeon: A sociable bird that forms tightly packed flocks on the mudflats and merse during the winter months. The colourful males have a distinctive '*wee-oo*' call, habitually uttered, with all the stress on the first note. (152)

Mallard: One or two fly up the glen to use ponds or even a quieter stretch of the burn, but they are more reliably found on the lochs and down in the bay on creeks running through the merse. (135)

Tufted duck: Can be difficult to find locally, but in summer Bengairn Loch, above the village, sometimes has a pair.

Scaup: This mollusc-eating seaduck can be a tricky bird to catch up with nationally, but the Solway is one of the best places to see it. Mostly it is found further east in the shallow waters of the inner firth, but the channel between Balcary Point and Hestan Island at the mouth of the bay sometimes supports a small flock. Usually, both sexes are present, with the striking males far more conspicuous on the water. (**75**)

Common scoter: The Solway is a vitally important site for this little black seaduck. Pick a day when the sea is calm and from a vantage point on the cliffs you'll have a good chance of finding them – usually packed together in flocks – on the water. Sometimes you'll even be able to hear them as they display to each other in small, mixed-sexed groups. In spring they migrate north to breed, but by late June some have already returned, so they can be found in good numbers (often many thousands) through most of the year. (**74–5, 85**)

Velvet scoter: A few birds tuck themselves away within the common scoter flocks, revealed (if not too distant) by their larger size, pale marks on the face and white patches on the folded wings. But picking them out is not easy. If you've had no luck, try homing in on birds that take to the air; the large white panels on the wings of a velvet scoter will now be obvious, even at a distance. (**75**)

Long-tailed duck: It's a dull January afternoon and two strikingly pale birds stand out as I pick through the hordes of scoters. Distant and lacking the long tails of the adult males, they brighten up my day nonetheless. I'll see what I take to be the same birds several times over the next few weeks, a little closer into the cliffs on one occasion. These are the only ones I've found.

Goldeneye: A compact, bright-eyed but shy duck that I've seen on just two occasions in winter, on Bengairn and Fellcroft Lochs. Each bird was diving so often that it spent most of its time out of sight, residing mostly within, rather than above, the water.

Goosander: A bird or two can turn up in the glen at any time of year, flying over or even trying to hunt down small fish along the burn, and a small flock is sometimes present on Fellcroft Loch in winter. A female seen on the burn in late April hinted at nesting, most likely in one of the old ash trees. Sure enough, in mid-May I found a brood of small young along the burn where it drains into the sea. (As an aside, the River Nith in Dumfries town centre is a reliable place to see this bird, allowing stunning close-up views as they fish below the weir.) (**145–6**)

The wildlife

Red-breasted merganser: One or two are seen along the coast in winter, usually close to the shore, but not always an easy bird to find locally.

Moorhen: The only non-duck to sneak into this section. It is scarce locally, but a few are present, year-round, on several of the lochs.

Gamebirds

Pheasant: A few wander up the glen from releases further afield. They become tame in the garden, and if you are too slow with the food they will stare in through the patio window, as if quietly challenging the idea that shooting one might be considered sport. (28, 106)

Red-legged partridge: Released for shooting, along with the more abundant pheasants, in the surrounding countryside but (unlike the pheasants) they don't find their way far up the glen. The closest I've seen one to the house was a lone bird singing its hoarse, chuntering song from the top of a stone dyke just above the cliffs. (78)

Red grouse: A few can still be found on the heather-clad slopes of Bengairn or unplanted moorland on the opposite side of the glen. It can be so long between sightings that I almost forget they are here – and then, unexpectedly, a pair will explode into the air ahead of me. The strange, nasal calls implore humans to 'go back – go back', as if it knows well our intentions towards gamebirds. (**118–19**, 122)

Divers and grebes

Red-throated diver: Seen regularly, though in small numbers, in winter along the coast, diving repeatedly into the murky waters after small fish. The mouth of the bay between Balcary Point and Hestan Island is a good spot, and here they often fish just a few metres away from the rocks, affording close-up views. From about April onwards they can be seen in the breeding plumage for which they were named. (**75**, 100)

Little grebe: A pair or two of these diminutive, fluffy grebes live on the loch nearest to the village. They dive frequently for food, popping back up to the surface like a cork after each brief underwater foray.

Great crested grebe: Our small freshwater lochs are, it would appear, too small to support a breeding pair, so I make do with the occasional wintering bird on the sea, where marine rather than freshwater fish keep them well fed.

Gannet, petrels and cormorants

Gannet: Birds from the huge colony on Ailsa Craig (and perhaps elsewhere) regularly wander into the Solway in summer, and can be watched from the cliffs. (4, **27–8**, **85**, 86, **153–4**)

Fulmar: Breeds in small numbers on flat, grassy patches on the sea-cliffs. Its long breeding season means that birds are present until late summer. Their nest sites are on inaccessible ledges, which is just as well; breeding birds spit a foul-smelling oil to deter intruders. (5, 78, 79, 80, 83)

Cormorant: When the tide is high I see a bird or two fishing in the bay, and it is very common at the cliffs, fishing offshore and flying up to ledges to roost overnight. The low cliffs on the seaward-facing side of Hestan Island support a colony of at least a few dozen pairs. (**75–6**, **96–7**, 100, 155)

Shag: Surprisingly difficult to find locally, especially in summer, though it breeds on cliffs and islands further west along the coast. But I sometimes come across a bird or two, either resting on rocks or fishing offshore. Once, a young shag chased a mackerel as I was reeling it in towards the rocks, leaving an imprint of its beak on the fish before (thankfully) relinquishing its grip. (86)

Herons and egrets

Grey heron: Usually seen down in the bay, picking off small fish from the shallows. The odd bird flaps lazily up into the glen to try its luck along the burn or one of the ponds. I accidentally flushed one from its catch when

The wildlife

walking along the burn one day: an immaculate, richly patterned brown trout no more than 12 centimetres long.

Little egret: A recent colonist that has spread north with the warming climate. I overlooked the first one I saw out in the bay, thinking it was a stray plastic bag, until it lifted into the air. Occasionally one flies up the burn, past the house – the white bird incongruous, somehow, against a backdrop of heather-clad hills. (155)

Birds of prey and owls

White-tailed eagle: This bird doesn't merit its place in the list as I've yet to see one here, but I couldn't resist. It has been seen along the coast not far from us, and thanks to the reintroduction programme, numbers are increasing. I don't think it'll be long before the local geese have one more thing to worry about, and I can enjoy the spectacle. (**122–3**)

Golden eagle: A bird that seems, somehow, to complete the place whenever it appears, which is all too infrequently. If you're looking out for one, watch for the mobbing behaviour of smaller birds of prey; if the local buzzards are diving at something that makes them look small and insignificant, then your luck just might be in. (**121–4**)

Red kite: One or two seen most days, anywhere from high above the slopes of Bengairn down to the fields by the house, where it hunts for worms. The woods near the house look perfect for breeding, but so far the mature, oak-dominated woods on Almorness Point are the only place I've found a nest. (3, 8, 12, **14–15**, 23, 26, 44, **68**, **93**, 121, 123, **125**, 161)

Buzzard: Britain's commonest raptor, and the one I see most often. The glen is excellent buzzard habitat, with open areas for hunting, a varied prey base, and plenty of mature trees in which to site the large stick nests. One year they nested close to the house, choosing one of the few conifers in a mainly deciduous wood. (8, 23, 26, 44, 121, 129)

Hen harrier: A bird with the knack for surprise. Absent for months and then, when you least expect it, there it is again. For my first sighting here, I happened to be looking out of the kitchen window at just the right time. A ring-tail (a young bird or an adult female) drifted by, wings held in that distinctive V as it pushed resolutely up the glen. This was mid-March, so perhaps it was heading from the coast towards a breeding site somewhere up in the Galloway hills. How long will it be before the next sighting I wonder?

Osprey: A well-known pair breeds on the Threave Estate, not too far from home, so it's a bird I look out for. Occasionally one passes through the glen. More often, I see them out in the bay. I watched one in late summer carry its catch across the mudflats, mobbed relentlessly by gulls, before settling on a low rock to feed. (**124–6**)

Sparrowhawk: The lightning-fast, one-word answer to the question: 'Why are the garden birds *always* so jumpy?' It keeps low to the ground when hunting, materialising close to the feeders and then vanishing again just as quickly, sometimes carrying away a bird that was not quite jumpy enough. (**107, 110**)

Goshawk: A buzzard-sized relative of the sparrowhawk and a fearsome predator of birds up to the size of pigeons and gamebirds. It often hunts within the forests and so can be difficult to see, but I chance upon one every so often, especially in late winter or early spring when they are more active in the airspace above the trees. (121)

Kestrel: Far from common, but I often see at least one on a long walk, hovering somewhere over the open, unplanted hills, wherever there is grass thick enough to hide voles and other small mammals. I also see them regularly along the cliffs, where breeding sites and good foraging habitat exist close together.

Merlin: A glimpse here and there of a tiny, sharp-winged falcon, on its way somewhere else, is all I've caught. But that's the merlin for you. If you are lucky enough to see one, watch it for as long as you possibly can; you never know how long it will be before the next opportunity arises.

The wildlife

Peregrine: There is a pair in the hills and another pair on the sea-cliffs, but adults can be seen hunting almost anywhere. I saw one trying (and failing) to catch a snipe. Another dived at lightning speed into a flock of swallows above the garden, before carrying one away into the hills, distraught hirundines trailing in its wake. Others try their luck with ducks or waders out in the bay, probing for weaknesses with low, fast flights out over the mudflats. (**16–17, 78, 83–4, 110, 125,** 151)

Barn owl: Common enough, though sightings are scarce. I came across a dead one on the edge of a forest track, and we occasionally hear their otherworldly screeches near the house after dark. Our neighbours at the head of the glen see them more regularly. They have a pair that uses a tree-mounted nest box close to their house. (**56, 87–8,** 129)

Tawny owl: A resident of the old woods, where a pair has reared young in a rotten alder for two years running. In autumn and winter they fill the darkness with sharp 'kee-wick' calls and soft, spine-tingling hoots. These sounds are sometimes borrowed to add atmosphere to films, and they do just the same for our glen. (25, 26, 28, **88,** 129, 143, 144)

Waders

Oystercatcher: Common in the bay, and impossible to miss with its striking pied plumage and shrill calls. Hundreds feed together, often close to the waterline, and the shingle beach on Hestan Island is a favoured high-tide roost. An occasional pair flies up the glen close to the house in spring. They don't stay, though breeding pairs can be found in the bay and by one of the larger lochs. (Delightfully, they nest on a roundabout and the roof of a Tesco superstore in the nearby town of Castle Douglas.)

Bar-tailed godwit: Common in winter on the Solway, but not always easy to find close to home. A few are sometimes present out in the bay, foraging along the edge of the sea or coastal creeks, with their long, gently upturned bills.

Black-tailed godwit: Unpredictable, but seen occasionally in the bay during passage periods on their way to or from their breeding grounds further north.

In spring, some have already developed their rich orange-rufous breeding colours.

Curlew: Common on the mudflats through most of the year, but especially so in winter. Sadly, it no longer breeds locally, though a few birds fly up the glen sometimes, to seek out fields with earthworms, bringing their magical, hauntingly wild cries up from the coast. (**7, 27**, 35, 45, **155**)

Whimbrel: Common enough in the bay on passage, when heading to or from its northern breeding grounds. Smaller than the similar curlew, with a shorter bill, pale lines on the crown and above the eye, and a loud, rippling whistle, 'pee-pee-pee-pee-pee', all on the same note. (155)

Knot: This mid-sized wader is a common winter visitor to the Solway's mudflats. Locally, though, it can be hard to find: it is often absent from the mudflats of the bay but small numbers drop in occasionally in winter, and during the spring and late summer passage periods.

Dunlin: A small, grey wader, scuttling here and there as it probes the mudflats for food, providing a striking contrast to the larger, more ponderous curlew, though (size apart) both share the same basic idea for a bill. In spring, before most head north to breed, it develops a black patch on the belly and is chestnut brown above.

Purple sandpiper: In winter, small groups can be found along the shore between Balcary and Rascarrel. It is surely our most stoical wader, shuffling unobtrusively about the rocks or resting with its head tucked into its feathers, ignoring the splashes from the waves breaking around it. Even humans are tolerated, allowing close-up views if you are willing to clamber out across slippery rocks. (The turnstone is another wader that enjoys low, seaweed-covered rocks and in most places is the more common of the two. I've seen it elsewhere on the Solway, but have yet to find it locally.)

Ringed plover: Small groups can be found on the mudflats at any time of year, often accompanied by dunlins. A pair or two try to breed on little sand and shingle beaches around the bay. Sadly, they choose the very places

The wildlife

that hold most appeal to people and their dogs, and disturbance can be a problem. (**93–4**)

Golden plover: An unpredictable bird here, sometimes found resting on the merse above the bay in small numbers in winter and occasionally flying through the glen in small, tightly packed flocks when commuting from one place to another.

Lapwing: I see small flocks around the edge of the bay in winter, or flying through the glen, though they always seem to move on quickly. Sadly, it no longer breeds locally. (7, 27, 45)

Redshank: One of a handful of wintering and passage waders which can be seen only with a trip down to the bay. Here loose groups of up to 20 birds probe into the soft mud for worms and tiny snails. Known for its high-pitched, excitable alarm calls when agitated: the 'sentinel of the marsh'. (27)

Common sandpiper: I've seen up to three migrants at a time along the shore of the bay in spring and autumn. Its compulsive tail-bobbing sometimes gives it away and, when disturbed, the escape flight is distinctive: low to the ground (or water) on stiffly flicked, erratic wing-beats.

Snipe: A few can usually be found in winter wherever there is waterlogged vegetation, including the edges of ponds and burns. When flushed, it can't resist a disgruntled call (like a stuck welly being pulled up from the mud), and what feels like a huge over-reaction as it zig-zags away into the distance. (7, 27, 45, **135–6**)

Jack snipe: 'Jack' is used here to mean 'small', and the bird is indeed smaller (and scarcer) than the similar snipe. The jack snipe flushes at close range, silently, then quickly dropping back into cover rather than disappearing into the distance. Sneaking up on one is a challenge, but worth it for the privileged close-up views. (**135–6**)

Woodcock: Britain's most abundant wintering wader, shunning wetlands for the woods and the hill country, and flighting out at dusk to probe the meadows with its long, flexible bill. Perfectly camouflaged in the leaf litter, it is revealed only by a startling clatter of wings should you inadvertently stray too close. (**136–7**)

Terns and gulls

Sandwich tern: An early migrant, one that can be seen from March onwards, patrolling the sea on the lookout for small fish near the surface. Small groups sometimes rest on the beach and their grating 'kirrick' calls are a giveaway whenever they rise into the air. Young birds with dark, scaly backs appear in late summer. (Other terns visit the Solway, but, so far, this is the only one I've seen locally.) (**85**)

Black-headed gull: Like most of its tribe these days, very much a gull, not just a seagull, roaming well inland in its quest for pastures rich in earthworms. Its sharply pointed wings with a white triangle on the leading edge set it apart from the slightly larger common gull. (**28**, 96)

Common gull: The second of the two smaller gulls we see regularly. Found along the shore, but also inland where it feeds on earthworms in the fields and, as with the other gulls, it often takes advantage of worms brought to the surface by slurry-spreading. Look for black-tipped wings with large white spots (or 'mirrors') near the tip. (**28**)

Great black-backed gull: Huge, dark-backed gull with a thuggish streak; not beyond swallowing smaller birds whole if the opportunity arises. Small numbers can be found down in the bay, or flying offshore off the cliffs at any time of year, and they nest around the rocky shoreline of Hestan Island. (**76**, **96**, **99**, **102**)

Lesser black-backed gull: Often found in large, mixed flocks of gulls, where food is abundant, or when passing through the glen, commuting between foraging areas. Breeds communally with the similar-sized herring gull on the grassy slopes of Hestan Island and the cliffs at Balcary. It can be hard to find in winter when most of the population has moved south to England or further afield. (**28**, **44**, 78, 83, **96**, 155)

The wildlife

Herring gull: The classic seaside gull, though it also roams well inland, bringing the sounds of the shore up into the glen as it patrols the fields, looking for earthworms. It breeds on grassy ledges on the cliffs, and its nests are dotted all over Hestan Island, from the shingle beaches to the sheep pastures above. (**28**, 44, **76**, 78, 81, **82**, 83, **96**, 98, 155)

Kittiwake: A refined and delicate seagoing gull, with the most indelicate of calls. It screams its name incessantly from the steep rocky breeding ledges that are occupied through the summer. Young birds have a distinctive black zig-zag across the wings in contrast to the plain black-tipped wings of the adults. (5, 78, 79, 80, **81**, **82**, 83)

Auks

Black guillemot: Hard to miss with its striking black-and-white plumage, bright red legs and habit of keeping close to the shoreline. A few pairs nest in the jumble of boulders and caves around the bottom of the sea-cliffs. (**79**, **83**)

Guillemot: Present at the breeding colonies on the cliffs from late winter until July/August when the young, still unable to fly efficiently, launch themselves into the sea below. As with the other auks, the odd bird may appear close to the cliffs at any time of year. (5, **78-9**, 80, **81-2**, **83**, 100)

Razorbill: Present along the cliffs in summer, and easier to watch than the guillemots because some of its nesting ledges are in full view of the clifftop footpath. Even at a distance it can be picked out of mixed groups of auks by looking for its thick, beautifully white-striped bill and jet-black, rather than muddy-brown, plumage. (5, **78–9**, 80, **81–2**, **83**, **86–7**, 100)

Cuckoo, pigeons and doves

Cuckoo: Its simple song is one of the most evocative sounds of summer, though it is increasingly hard to come by further south in Britain. Here, though, it is still common, and birds sing at each other incessantly across the glen as males seek out a willing female. Pipits and other small birds, beware. (34, **65**, **80–1**, **170**)

Collared dove: A bird that keeps us close, favouring gardens and settlements. It is most noticeable down in the village, on wires and chimney pots, watching humanity pass by below. (26)

Stock dove: A smaller, more refined and more delicate version of the woodpigeon. It feeds out in the open and conceals its stick nest (and two white eggs) in holes in old trees or buildings.

Woodpigeon: Flocks of up to a few dozen frequent the woods or pass through the glen. And the soft, gentle song is a soporific soundtrack to summer. It builds flimsy, often barely functioning, nests in small trees and bushes, the two white eggs sometimes visible through the structure from below. (106, 118)

Rock dove: Common along the sea-cliffs where it breeds in caves. Some look like the original, wild-type birds, but genetic evidence shows that there has been significant interbreeding with escaped and free-living feral pigeons. (**79**)

Feral pigeon: Small flocks around farm buildings involve stray racing pigeons and their descendants, with the birds exhibiting a bewilderingly diverse array of plumage types. (79)

Kingfisher and woodpeckers

Kingfisher: It wasn't until September of our second autumn here that I finally caught up with this bird. It was perched, jewel-like, above a small, dark pool, tucked away within scrub and trees near Almorness Point. Whenever I walk along the Hass Burn near home I look out for it there too, but in vain up to now.

Great spotted woodpecker: A flexible, adaptable bird that has spread north into Galloway. It raids the garden for nuts, even taking the hazelnuts we put out for the squirrels, carrying them away to wedge in a tree crevice so they can be cracked open. Its nest holes in old trees in the woods are best found by looking out for little piles of wood chips on the ground below. (26, 106, 144)

The wildlife

Green woodpecker: The distinctive laughing call is a common enough sound in summer. It nests in the woods and forages for ants (using its long, sticky tongue) in the old, flower-rich meadows nearby. (**47**, 144)

Larks, pipits and wagtails

Skylark: Much of the farmland at lower levels is managed too intensively for skylarks, and land smothered with conifers quickly becomes unsuitable. But this iconic bird is still common enough in the hills; wherever there is thick, tussocky grass, it can be heard pouring out its song from the air above. (7, 118)

Grey wagtail: It turns up in ones and twos along the burn, by the manure heap in the old quarry, even by the garden pond occasionally, constantly pumping its long, elegant tail. But it tends not to stay in one place for long, and I have yet to find a local breeding site.

Pied wagtail: A bird drawn to hard surfaces, on one day found along the lane by the cemetery, and on another down in the village or, fleetingly, on the roof of our garage. Like its more elegant relative (above) it fans out its long tail to help it brake rapidly and change direction during its frenetic pursuits of insects.

Rock pipit: Larger and darker than the other pipits, and very much tied to the coast. In interludes when there is little activity offshore, I watch them flying about the sea-cliffs, and this is a good place to compare it to the smaller and more common meadow pipit. Along the shore, it seeks out piles of washed-up, rotting seaweed where invertebrates are abundant. (**77**, 84)

Meadow pipit: Common and widespread in open areas of the hill country, including large clearings, as well as at lower levels and along the coast. Occasionally, a bird flushing at close range will reveal its nest site, cleverly concealed deep inside a tussock of grass. In winter it can turn up almost anywhere, in small, lively flocks. (118, **156**, **162**)

Tree pipit: Summer visitor, from mid-April onwards, to clear-fells within the plantations, where there is plenty of bare ground, often perching on old stumps or piles of brash to sing. It must move on when the newly planted trees become too tall and dense, but that's no problem – there is always another clear-fell. (**24**, 55, 65)

Swift, swallows and martins

Swift: It breeds, we think, in the village (as well as in the local towns), but higher up the glen its visits are erratic and unpredictable. Swifts follow their aerial food supply, even high into the hills when conditions are right. It is the ultimate master of the skies, mating, eating and even sleeping on the wing. Young birds, once fledged, may not land again for several years, until they nest. (87, **118**)

Sand martin: One of the earliest migrants to return each spring. It excavates nest tunnels in the sides of a small quarry near the house. The adults perch on wires, and delight us by sweeping gracefully through the garden with the more abundant swallows and house martins, hunting flying insects. (43, **105**)

House martin: Common in summer, building its mud nests under the eaves of houses in the village. One year a pair started to build on our house but soon gave up. Hopefully, one day soon, they might finish the job. (43, 110)

Swallow: In early April we slide the garage doors open a few centimetres for the summer – that's all the swallows need. They also nest in one of the sheds, flying in through a window where the glass is missing. I often watch them weaving their low flights between the cows, where flies become concentrated. (**33**, **43**, 78, 105, **109–10**, 111)

Dipper, waxwing and dunnock

Dipper: Found along the Hass Burn. Close to the house, it's an unpredictable visitor. But it breeds on a footbridge down in the village where the burn is wider. In late April, I watched them nest-building, dipping moss into the water before adding it to a nest tucked out of sight beneath the bridge. Unknowing human feet regularly pass just a few centimetres above. (Away from the glen, I often see them along the river in Dalbeattie town centre, where I think they must nest.) (24)

The wildlife

Waxwing: I'm afraid I'm going to cheat with this one. Even though our second winter here was a waxwing winter and I scanned the berry bushes in the glen dutifully on every walk, it was not to be. For some reason, it is urban areas that appeal most strongly to this bird, and a pre-Christmas shopping trip to Dumfries, 20 miles away, did the trick. The birds were shunning the abundant yellow rowan berries and instead were fly-catching from the tops of the tallest trees in the park.

Dunnock: Often known as the hedge sparrow, in fact this is the only British representative of the accentor family. It ekes out a living unobtrusively, wherever there is low cover, and while it is not the most brightly coloured or expressive of birds, it is well known among ornithologists for its varied and colourful sex life. (55)

Chats and thrushes

Robin: Sings through the winter, adding welcome texture to the landscape during the quieter months. With its big eyes it is often the last songbird to be active each day as the light fades. We once watched *seven* together around the patio during a cold snap. Although they were sparring with each other, they were forgoing the usual territorial fights as they were all so desperate to feed. (2, **23–4**, 44, 62, 77)

Stonechat: A show-off, perching at the very top of plant stems and bushes, from where it launches itself after invertebrate prey. In summer, pairs are common enough in the hills and along the coast, and it remains with us through the winter. Its calls – like two stones being tapped together – give it away on the rare occasions when it is hidden from view. (2, 55, 118, **155–6**)

Whinchat: Not an easy bird to find here, but areas of rough, tussocky grass and bracken are always worth checking, especially in spring and autumn. In mid-May I came across a lovely male singing from its perch on a deer fence, on the boundary between moorland and a young conifer plantation. (**163**)

Wheatear: An odd-sounding name for a bird that eats invertebrates and avoids crops. It's actually a modification of 'white arse' (after the flashy white rump), softened to avoid offending sensibilities. Much of the hill country here is too well vegetated to be ideal for them, but I see a few in places with rocky outcrops and plenty of bare ground. Other than along the cliffs, they are mostly passing through rather than staying on to breed.

Redstart: I suspect they breed in the old oaks and ash trees around Almorness Point. Closer to home, I see them mostly in late summer, passing through before they head south for the winter. The 'start' in the name is from the old English for 'tail', a feature that the bird advertises keenly, habitually vibrating it and exposing the orange-red feathers. (25, 26, 36, 53, 93, 109)

Black redstart: I've been lucky with this bird over the years and I was delighted to find a male here towards the end of November – a typical date for a migrant in this species. It was flying exuberant, fiery-tailed sorties after prey along a track near an old quarry, just a few hundred metres from home. It stayed for one more day before moving on.

Song thrush: A few remain with us through the winter, and the distinctive song can be heard from early in the New Year – strident short phrases, each repeated two to three times, ringing out brightly from a high vantage point. (27, 44, 106, 145)

Blackbird: With us year-round, in gardens and woodlands alike, offering up an object lesson in how ubiquity dulls appreciation. We take this bird for granted, though its rich, melodic song is surely unsurpassed. If it were rare, how far might we travel to hear one? (44, 145)

Mistle thrush: Present all year, and difficult to miss because of its harsh rattling calls. Most noticeable in late summer when adults and young gather together in loose flocks of up to 20 to 30 birds.

Fieldfare: With us from October to at least March, flocking and 'chakking' its way across the fields (for worms) and along the hedges (for berries), hundreds at a time in a good year. (The photo at the beginning of this section shows a bird that hit one of our windows but made a full recovery and flew off to rejoin its flock.) **(44)**

The wildlife

Redwing: Another gregarious thrush which, along with the fieldfare, heralds the onset of winter. It sports a jaunty pale eye-stripe and that lovely flush of red on the flanks. Often outnumbered by fieldfares locally, but common enough in the fields and hedges. (68)

Ring ouzel: This one still smarts a little. Our neighbours at the head of the glen sent us a photograph of a lovely young male perched in a small conifer in their garden. This was in early October and no doubt it was passing through on its way south for the winter. Sadly, it did not stick around for long.

Warblers

Blackcap: One of the commonest warblers in summer. Black-headed males sing their loud, fluty songs from the woods and patches of scrub, while the brown-capped females skulk in thick cover. A few appear in the garden, especially in autumn when they raid our rowan tree for berries. (25, 26, 34, 53, 65, 145)

Garden warbler: A late-arriving migrant, and a bird that can be difficult to see. It is much less common than the blackcap, being restricted to places where trees and bushes provide the thick cover it needs. The song lacks the blackcap's loud, exuberant flourishes, but often comes in longer bursts, giving the observer an opportunity to track down the singer. (65, **93**)

Whitethroat: Arrives in April to sing its scratchy song from tangles of low vegetation, especially brambles and along overgrown hedgerows. The edge of forest tracks and clear-fells are good places to look, as here there is enough light for dense natural vegetation to become established. (53, 65)

Lesser whitethroat: This one almost got away. Two years of living here, the book almost done … and then there it was: that unmistakable scratchy warble running into a louder, rapid rattle of harder notes. A few extra words to write after all. This was in late April but I hope it will stay to breed, and the habitat looks good – a patch of dense hawthorn, elder and gorse just above the merse.

Sedge warbler: Its lively, rapid-fire song rings out from the fringes of the reedbed above the merse from late April through the early part of the summer, mixing scratchy, buzzing sections with mimicry and more harmonious interludes. It favours the places where scrubby bushes occur at the landward edge of the reeds.

Chiffchaff: Less common here than its close relative the willow warbler, but the simple, two-note song can be heard from woodland throughout the glen. One of the earliest migrants to return in the spring. (65)

Willow warbler: A declining migrant in southern Britain, but doing very well in Galloway, singing its gentle, down-slurred cascade of notes from April onwards, wherever trees or bushes provide cover. It is one of the enduring sounds of the summer, heard on almost every walk. (25, 26, 53, 62, 65, 145)

Goldcrest and wren

Goldcrest: Tiny and easy to overlook (especially with my poor hearing) but common enough in woodland and scrub. One of a small handful of birds that is doing very well in the new plantations. (52, 68)

Wren: Wherever there is low cover, there's a good chance a wren will be close by, creeping about, mouse-like among the branches and foliage. Though unless it sings or starts up with its harsh, scolding calls, you may be none the wiser. (**23**, 55, 68)

Flycatchers

Pied flycatcher: When the ornithologist Bryan Nelson lived at Mine House not so long ago, he found this bird in the adjacent woods in summer. They are no longer here, which is a sad loss indeed. (25, 26, 27, 36, 109)

Spotted flycatcher: Fairly common in summer around the margins of woodland. A drab-looking bird but with a watchable, high-energy feeding behaviour. It launches erratic aerial sorties after flying insects from a branch or post, often landing back at the precise spot it took off from.

The wildlife

Tits, nuthatch and treecreeper

Blue tit: Up to ten at a time gather around our garden feeders, and a pair nest each year in an old cherry tree by the garage, rearing bundles of fluffy, yellow-faced fledglings that roam the summer garden. (**107**, 109)

Great tit: Common and easily found wherever trees and shrubs provide cover, and a frequent garden visitor. (109)

Coal tit: An adaptable little bird that does well in the plantations up in the hills, as well as the deciduous woods of the glen, caching food to help it through the winter. (There are no marsh tits here, and the scarce willow tit is found no nearer than the Threave Estate; so every brownish tit with a dark head is a coal tit.) (26, 52, 106)

Long-tailed tit: Sociable, lively flocks of up to about a dozen are a feature of winter. They are constantly on the move, swarming over the garden feeders for a few minutes before heading back to the woods. In spring they divide up into pairs and seek thick cover, especially brambles, to hide their remarkable barrel-shaped nests. (144)

Nuthatch: A jaunty acrobat of a bird, the only one able to scuttle head-first down a trunk. A recent colonist of Galloway, but already it is common in the woods and a bold raider of garden peanuts. Dominant in interactions with most small birds because of its powerful nut-cracking bill. (26, 27, 106, 145, 146)

Treecreeper: Unobtrusive, tree-coloured scaler of trunks in the woods, and a garden visitor that jerks its way up our apple trees, fence posts and even the roughcast coating of our garage.

Crows (corvids)

Raven: A bird that rarely disappoints, firing out its strange 'gronking' calls, always ready to turn a trick or two in the air, showing off to others of its own kind. One year a pair nested on a ledge on the sea-cliffs. Closer to home, I witnessed one of our local pairs attacking a cast sheep on the far side of the glen in late winter, one bird at the front of the animal, the other behind. I was too far away to intervene but contacted the farmer to tell him what was happening. 'Devil birds,' he muttered, and while I don't share his view, I now understand it. (11, **16**, 80, 118, 161)

Rook: There is a small rookery near the farm and a larger one in the village, strung out across numerous gardens that host the mature trees they need. Groups of birds regularly fly past the house heading for nearby fields in their relentless quest for invertebrates or, in autumn, to pull acorns from the canopy in the woods before flying back down the glen to hide them.

Carrion crow: Pairs dotted here and there through the glen, building their sturdy nests in the canopy of deciduous trees. In winter it sometimes joins up with other crows in fields with a good food supply or down on the shore at low tide. It is much persecuted because of its perceived impacts on gamebirds and lambs, so tends to be wary around humans. (44, **154**)

Hooded crow: Very scarce locally, and because it regularly interbreeds with the carrion crow, even birds with a lot of grey in the plumage may be hybrids. I watched a good-looking candidate flying north over the sea towards Hestan Island. If it was indeed a pure-bred hooded crow, perhaps it had come from the Isle of Man (visible in the distance), where it is common.

Jackdaw: Uses holes in the old ash trees for its untidy nests of sticks, and forages across the open farmland throughout the glen. (44, 77, 80, 144)

Magpie: Rather scarce here. Apart from a few family groups in late summer it's unusual to get past 'sorrow' or 'joy' in the well-known rhyme. Always wary of humans (with good reason), so not an easy bird to get close to. Even our occasional garden visitors remain on perpetual high alert.

Jay: Small groups haunt the woods, throwing hoarse screams back and forth between birds, flopping from tree to tree on short, rounded wings, and hunting for nuts in autumn. A frequent if cautious visitor to the garden. Like the other corvids, it seems keenly aware of the long, bloody history between humanity and its own kind. (**106**, 147)

The wildlife

Starling and sparrows

Starling: Energetic, tightly packed flocks roam the glen in winter, and again in midsummer when the distinctive, grey-plumaged young have fledged. But they are fickle birds. One day there will be hundreds in fields by the house, and the next day none.

House sparrow: Underappreciated due to its abundance and drab plumage, though as it declines so we come to value it more highly – such is human nature. Playful, noisy flocks stick close to houses and farms, though we see 'our' birds less frequently in early autumn, presumably because they are finding more food in the surrounding countryside at this time. And 'drab' – really? In spring the males are anything but. (24, 106)

Tree sparrow: An enigmatic and unpredictable bird, easy to overlook among flocks of its more common relative. Every so often, one or two will spend a few days visiting the garden before vanishing again for months. They must breed somewhere locally, though I have yet to find the place.

Finches and buntings

Chaffinch: The short, staccato song, rounded off with a joyful flourish, is one of the dominant sounds of summer, made by a bird as at home in the woods and young plantations as it is in village gardens – they are 'diminutive engines of cheerfulness' suggested writer Dominic Couzens, capturing them perfectly. Further south in Britain numbers have fallen dramatically, but they remain abundant here, at least for now. (26, 52, 106, 108)

Brambling: An unpredictable winter visitor that I always look for among the more familiar and abundant chaffinches, so far without much luck. A lone female is the only one I've seen. It was an occasional visitor to the garden through one winter, flashing its trademark white rump every time it flew up from the food.

Greenfinch: Nationally this bird has suffered from disease outbreaks, and is less common than it once was. A few visit the garden, always far outnumbered by the chaffinches. I see this bird more often in and around the village, singing and song-flighting from bushes in the spring. (**108**)

Goldfinch: Lively, twittering charms of goldfinches are common enough, taking sunflower seeds from the garden or seeking out wild corners where thistles and other plants have been left for long enough to set seed. (106)

Linnet: I see a bird or two along the hedgerows, in patches of gorse, or in one of the clear-fells where plants have had a chance to grow and set seed. But it is most common along the coast, wherever bushes and more open areas with abundant wild flowers occur close together.

Redpoll: Sometimes found in mixed flocks with siskins, especially in downy birch and alder trees, which both birds visit to feed on the small seeds. A few come to the garden feeders for sunflower hearts, again often mixing with siskins.

Siskin: A tiny, dapper bird. The yellow, green and black males brighten towards the breeding season as pale feather fringes are worn away. They do well in the plantations but often visit gardens when natural food is in short supply, especially in late winter and early spring. (3, 13, 26, 52)

Bullfinch: A pair here and there on the edges of woodland and patches of scrub. Plump, bright red males keep company with the duller brown females. Unless you have regular garden visitors, the best way to find this bird is by tuning into its discreet but distinctive melancholy whistle. (144)

Crossbill: A bird that has lived up to its reputation for being tricky to find. My poor hearing doesn't help, making it difficult to pick out the distinctive 'chip … chip … chip' calls. Or perhaps they just haven't been around much. When I finally got lucky, I couldn't have been more surprised. A female and juvenile were perched in a mature ash tree before flying down into a scrubby hawthorn. They must have strayed from the nearby spruce plantation, but away from the conifers they seemed oddly out of place.

The wildlife

Reed bunting: An occasional garden visitor, especially in cold weather, but found more commonly in damper areas with bushes and small trees, both along the coast and up in the hills.

Yellowhammer: Scarce locally, as expected for a bird that prefers arable or mixed farmland rather than landscapes dominated by pasture. At the end of winter a lone bird coming for seed was a welcome, if slightly incongruous, sight in the garden.

* * *

Birdwatching is popular not because birds are any more special than our other wild animals. Rather, it's a numbers game. Wherever you are in Britain (or, for that matter, in most of the world), there are about the right number of birds, of about the right number of species, to make a keen interest worthwhile: not so many that finding – and identifying – them all becomes daunting, but not so few that seeing them all is too trivial a task. The list above includes 138 birds that I've seen within walking distance of the house over the past two years or so. I still occasionally stumble into a new one (lesser whitethroat only just made the book) and I can expect more new additions in future, albeit at an ever-declining rate.

    The other vertebrates have no less appeal. Mammals, especially, show far more diversity in size, shape and behaviour than birds; you could make a strong case that they are the more varied and interesting group. The trouble is, they are thin on the ground. And many of them are frustratingly difficult to see, emerging only after dark, hiding away beneath the vegetation, or even disappearing into the soil itself. In a short walk from the house, I'll see (or hear) at least 20 species of bird, and on a good day in early summer it might be more than double that. On the same walk, there will be days when I won't encounter a single vertebrate of any other kind.

    All of which is a roundabout way of introducing the list below, and making clear that it is no mere afterthought. If I had to rank the handful of animals that bring me most pleasure, I would lean heavily on the creatures below. The garden-visiting red squirrel and badger might just make the number one and two spots. Pine marten would be near the top, even though we've only ever seen a single animal. And I'd willingly trade a few of our garden birds to keep the pipistrelles that move in with us for a few months each summer, and swarm out from under the eaves every evening.

First up is a creature with a special gift that no bird can match.

Reptiles

Adder: I don't see it often, but Galloway is a stronghold for adders and I always look out for them, especially on dry slopes with heather and bracken. It's the only creature here (these days) that can elicit just a hint of fear and it helps keep my senses heightened and 'in the moment'. I scan carefully ahead when walking, and I'm careful about where I put my hands when scrambling up a slope or finding a spot to sit down. (**18, 59**)

Common lizard: It lives up to its name in the hills, though unless your eyes are sharp, a flash of disappearing tail may be all that you see. A long summer walk will usually turn up a few in good weather. Hazel enjoyed the best sighting: a demonstration of its dramatic defence against predators, and a case of two for the price of one. (**59**, 130)

Slow worm: This creature, a legless lizard, is all too easy to overlook. I've only found it in one place, under stones fallen from a dyke at the edge of an old, ant-rich pasture. If curiosity hadn't prompted me to lift up a stone or two, I'd have been none the wiser. (46)

Amphibians

Common frog: From February onwards clumps of spawn appear wherever there is lying water. The smaller the pool, the less chance that predators will be present to threaten the eggs or tadpoles, though the greater the risk of drying out. The animal itself is not always easy to see (much activity occurs after dark) though it is common enough around the garden.

Common toad: The humble toad has a charm and character all its own. We see it often in the garden, and it breeds in the pond in spring, when its typical calm, stoic demeanour suddenly changes. Groups of males grab any female they can find, forming writhing balls. Soon afterwards, long, dark strings of eggs appear in the water, far less obvious than the common frog's clumps of spawn. One local cattle grid acts as a pitfall trap, with unclimbable vertical sides, so I've installed a little ramp of stones. (**107–8, 154**)

Natterjack toad: The coastal fringes of the Solway are a stronghold for this rare animal. It has specialist habitat requirements, favouring sand dunes and heathland, which we don't have in our glen. So a short late-evening excursion by car is required to have a chance of seeing it.

Palmate newt: Our garden pond supports dozens of this, our smallest newt, from early spring right through the summer, and I see them regularly in ponds up in the hills. In moorland and hill country with acidic conditions, this is the newt you are most likely to find. (108)

Mammals

Roe deer: The only deer we've seen here, though deer-stalkers tell us that sika and red deer visit the local hills occasionally. (Wild goats, too, occur elsewhere in the Galloway hills, but not here.) Roe deer stick to small groups, and six is the most I've seen together. They roam widely through all types of habitat, even using the reedbed above the bay, and it's unusual not to see any on a long walk. If you hear what sounds like a dog barking in remote country where dogs rarely go, this animal will be the culprit. (23, 43, 56, **66**, 130, 143)

Wild boar: I'm including this species for two reasons. Firstly, it's well known that they have become established in parts of Galloway following escapes from captivity. And secondly, the people who lived here before us found one under our garden hedge one day. So I keep a lookout. The turf-turning capabilities of our local badgers have got my hopes up a few times (mimicking the signs of rooting that are typical of boar), but that's as close as I've come.

Lynx: Long gone from Britain, along with a dispiriting array of other large mammals, but our glen – specifically the hill country above Auchencairn – is a significant footnote to the story. According to recent evidence this may have been the last place in Britain that the lynx was found, clinging on into the 18th century, much later than previously thought. Perhaps, then, these hills, with their extensive forests, few roads and abundant roe deer, would be a good place to begin its restoration; a case of last out, first back in. (**14**, 63)

Fox: Much less common here than the badger. Fears about predation of lambs mean that numbers are kept down. But I see foxes regularly enough, and the well-vegetated hills and plantations provide a refuge that is safer than the farmland below. Last May, a small cub regularly ventured out into a field by the house in daylight. It looked too small to be out unattended, and we wondered what fate might have befallen its parents. (8, 23, 43, 44, 66, 130, 131, 143)

Pine marten: We were spoiled by an unexpected appearance soon after we moved in. There it was, on the patio by the sliding doors, peering in through the glass in the fading light. It moved confidently – as if it had been here before, we thought. Surely, we would see it regularly. Well, not a bit of it. Since then, I've had to make do with finding the thin, twisted droppings on forest tracks up in the hills. It would be lovely to see another, but, for now, just knowing they are here is enough. (**8**, **17**, **35**, 130)

Badger: A common, adaptable mammal that roams all parts of the glen after dark, including the hill slopes as well as the farmland and woodland below. Its well-worn paths lead from setts hidden in the trees, and connect up all of these habitats. Dung pits are everywhere, marking out territories. We are lucky that they grace our patio with their presence every evening, sometimes in daylight. Without these regular visitors, years could easily slip by without seeing one. (8, 23, 44, 66, **108**, 130, 131, 144, 148)

Otter: Our neighbours at the head of the valley caught one on camera as it paid a night-time visit to their pond, and I've found spraint on rocks at the edge of the burn near the house. But I've seen it in the flesh only along the coast, including Hestan Island, as well as the rocky shoreline near Balcary Point, fishing close to the rocks. I watched one swim the channel between the mainland and Hestan Island, a little under a mile away, to forage in the rocky inlets around the island. (**100**, **101–2**)

Stoat: It pains me to admit it, but this creature has eluded me. More painful still is the fact that Hazel has seen one in the garden. And in case I was tempted

The wildlife

to doubt her eyes, our neighbours have photographic proof from their front lawn. The local countryside looks ideal with all its woods, hedges and dykes, though perhaps the lack of rabbits, a key prey species, explains why it is not more common (see below).

Rabbit: Surprisingly, rabbits are missing from the upper part of glen around the house, though they are common enough in fields down by the village, tucking their burrows away beneath dense gorse bushes. Did an outbreak of disease wipe them out, perhaps, and if so, will they gradually spread back? (98)

Brown hare: This animal has been with us for so long we tend to regard it as an honorary native, and it is doing well here, one day lolloping across the fields, another racing along the farm track ahead of the car, or hiding out in the woods. Hazel saw one on the beach, and we regularly flush both adults and youngsters from the garden flowerbeds. (Mountain hares don't occur locally, but further into the Galloway hills they too can be found.) (**23**, **43**, **47**, **130**, **131**, **144**)

Common and soprano pipistrelle: We have other bats too. (The Threave Estate, not many miles away, has eight species, including the rare whiskered bat.) When we have ventured out from the house after dark with the bat detector we've picked up signals from noctules, brown long-eared and Daubenton's bats. But it's these two (only recently recognised as separate species) that we share our summer with. Hundreds of them occupy wall spaces and gaps under the roof tiles, flying out each evening just as we are settling in for the night. One (a common pipistrelle) strayed into our living room through an open window, requiring a delicate catch-and-release operation to free it. (**109–12**)

Hedgehog: An occasional flattened mat of spines appears on the road that passes through the village, so we know they are here, despite the high numbers of badgers – a known hedgehog predator. We have yet to bump into a live hedgehog, though.

Mole: Common in the fields though less so in late winter, after the mole-catcher has done his rounds. Our garden, the woods and the hill country above the farm dyke provide a refuge and supply willing recruits for the inevitable recolonisation. The closest I've ever come to seeing one here was the twitching soil of a molehill. I waited silently, frozen with anticipation for several minutes, but it was not to be. (**131**)

Common shrew: I can't hear their squeaks any more, so I know they're here only through the odd glimpse in the undergrowth and an occasional dead one. The slightly smaller pygmy shrew is probably here too, but when I've measured the body-to-tail ratio and checked the distinctive red-tipped teeth in the upper jaw, the dead ones have always been common shrews.

Wood mouse: Common in the woods, where I find the neatly-holed hazelnut shells they leave behind, and in the garden where animals emerge at dusk to run entertaining shuttles – half-running, half-jumping – between cover and nuts on the patio, sometimes dodging between the badgers. We hear them scurrying around in the loft and the wall spaces, and every so often one finds its way into the living area until ushered out again inside a Longworth (live catch) trap. (129)

Field vole: Our pets let us know there are voles around, our dog frantically trying to excavate their nests in thick tussocks of grass or under stones, until dragged reluctantly away. The cat goes a step further. He is not a prolific hunter, but brings in the occasional short-tailed, blunt-nosed body. In the bay I've watched as voles have fled from an especially high tide that inundated the rough grassland above the shoreline. (**154**)

Bank vole: A rarely seen denizen of our flowerbeds and no doubt other areas with sufficient cover. Occasionally I see one running daring daylight shuttles from cover to steal bird food from the lawn or patio. It has a slightly longer tail than the field vole, a reddish tint to the fur and ears that are a little more obvious. (129)

Brown rat: Along with the house mouse, this species is missing from much of Galloway. Large areas of upland and plantation are unsuitable, and farmsteads and settlements are thinly spread, so commensal species may struggle to maintain a presence; once lost from a site, recolonisation may be difficult. Rats are present on Hestan Island, where dead gulls pulled down into holes could

The wildlife

only have been their work. A skull found in the garden and old tins of poison at the back of the shed suggest that they were once here too. (99)

Red squirrel: After a lifetime of grey squirrels, what a joy it is to live in a place where our hard-pressed native squirrel brightens up the local woods. They take nuts from the patio, and if the food runs out one might put its front paws up against the glass, as if asking for more. In autumn they disappear from the garden and can be found (with luck) only in the woods. Why? Because fresh, wild hazelnuts are a cut above handouts from humans. (3, 13, 24, **31–6**, **108**, 130, 144, **146**, 147)

Grey squirrel: This is an animal we take no pleasure in seeing. It's not their fault, of course, but they spread a disease to which they have immunity but which kills red squirrels. So when one appears in the garden, a hardening of hearts is required, and out comes the air rifle; so far five have been killed, and it seems inevitable that there will be more to deal with. (**31**, 33–5)

Grey seal: I see one occasionally close to the cliffs at Balcary Point or from Hestan Island. They are usually invisible in the churned, muddy waters but look for a bull-nosed head sticking above the surface as the animal comes up to breathe and to survey its surroundings. (Common seals occur less frequently in the Solway, and I've yet to see one.) (**100**)

Harbour porpoise: Small and unobtrusive, but present in the Solway year-round and easy enough to see from the cliffs when the sea is calm, especially when they are close to shore. They surface briefly (but often) when all that is visible is the dark, rounded back and little triangular dorsal fin. (84, **100**)

Bottle-nosed dolphin: They turn up every so often in summer, offshore of the cliffs at Balcary. They are larger and far more demonstrative than porpoises, sometimes leaping clear of the water. (Other dolphins and even whales enter the Solway from time to time, but they are unpredictable; the luck required to see them has eluded me so far.) (**84–5**)

Fish

Brown trout: There is just this one freshwater fish on the list – but what a creature it is, lurking in the pools of the burn, hanging motionless in the current or darting away at such speed the human eye can scarcely keep up. The spots on the flanks and the subtle variations in pattern and colour always invite a closer look. And so I lie down at the edge of the burn, head overhanging the bank, to watch them. (6, 146)

Mackerel: Easy to catch in summer from the cliffs wherever a line can be cast into deep water; few other fish snap at the lure more impulsively. This small fish provides food for the larger seabirds, especially gannets, as well as fish-eating mammals, so its presence is very welcome to them as well as to us: freshly caught and cooked the same day, no other fish tastes quite as good. (153)

Thornback ray: Also known as 'roker' by commercial fishermen. A large kite-shaped fish with a long, spiny tail and flattened body, which also has spines or 'thorns'. It seems to be abundant in our part of the Solway, based on the frequency with which I've seen sea-anglers haul them up onto the rocks. Some are returned carefully to the water, but the wings are apparently good to eat. (152)

Dogfish: The local sea-anglers catch the lesser spotted dogfish (a type of small shark) regularly, often throwing them back, though they can be eaten; dogfish (also, confusingly, known as cat sharks) are sometimes served in chippies as 'rock salmon', to make them sound more appealing. On the shingle beach near the hotel, I once found a dogfish lying motionless but alive on the high-tide line. It was 3 feet long and so may have been the larger greater-spotted dogfish. I carried it gently down to the retreating sea (skin rough as sandpaper), and it slipped sluggishly away through the shallows. (152, **153–5**)